THE MOMENTUM
BLUEPRINT:
UNLOCKING
SUCCESS
THROUGH RESILIENCE

STRATEGIES FOR BUILDING
UNSTOPPABLE SUCCESS

THE MOMENTUM BLUEPRINT: UNLOCKING SUCCESS THROUGH RESILIENCE

STRATEGIES FOR BUILDING UNSTOPPABLE SUCCESS

BY: ROB SPERRY

TGON Publishing

TGON Publishing

CONTENTS

FOREWORD 9

1   **INTRODUCTION**   11

2   **JOHN & KRISTI OAKEY**   15

3   **RICKY DURANT**   23

4   **LEAH LOCKETT**   31

5   **AMBER GUSTOWSKI**   39

6   **JENNIFER (JENN) GLACKEN**   47

7   **SHELLY TAYLOR**   57

8   **CORRINA D'ALESSIO**   65

9   **LOUISE GATLAND**   75

10   **SHANNON HOWARD**   87

11   **DORA EDMONSON**   97

12 **KIM WARD** 107

13 **MATT HALL** 115

14 **ASHLEY DAWES** 123

15 **ALESHA LIMBO** 131

16 **EDIE LABELLE** 139

17 **MAUREEN MESSMER** 147

18 **RACHAEL LALJI** 157

19 **BRENT ORWELL** 163

20 **CHRISTINE RYDZIK** 171

21 **TARA PAGE TRUAX** 179

FOREWORD

Momentum. Let's talk about Momentum. I have been blessed to be a part of and witness momentum in companies and people over the last 20 years of coaching high performers and being one myself.

The most critical momentum is NOT the one you wish your company were in, where sales, flying, and ranks are broken at breakneck speeds, but the momentum of YOU growing through your daily habits and disciplines.

In the last 15 years, I have gone from losing it all in the real estate crash to building an Inc 5000 company that has generated over $30 million, became a #1 earner in a network marketing company, become a multiple best-selling author, and have trained teams all over the world. And all of this having come from a broken and abusive home, not graduating high school on time, and not having hardly any advantages in life but just choosing to work hard and have discipline.

I can tell you that personal development and self-development are HARD. I have invested well over a million dollars in my education through masterminds, coaches, events, and courses, but the greatest source of my growth, BY FAR, was in 2022, when I turned to and found God.

I didn't grow up in the church, and later, I would learn that how we feel about our biological father is also how we feel about our Heavenly Father. I thought God was mean and uncaring, and He would never be proud of me,e and I would never be good enough because that is how I felt about my biological dad.

The truth is that God loves you, and His nature is always to grow you. My best source to maintain momentum in my life now is to trust God, be in His word daily, and constantly thank Him for being with me, guiding me, and helping me.

All growth became more manageable when I turned to my Heavenly Father, and it will be for you, too, if you choose. Now, enjoy this book and see what God wants you to learn from it, as my friend Rob has masterfully put together a powerful resource to help YOU and your team get into massive momentum!

Ray Higdon
Author - The Faith Driven Network Marketer

INTRODUCTION

Whether you're in network marketing or any form of entrepreneurship, one thing is certain—growth isn't optional. Success isn't about luck, timing, or the perfect circumstances. It's about who you become in the process. It's about resilience, leadership, and taking relentless action even when the odds seem stacked against you.

This book isn't just for those in network marketing—it's for anyone looking to elevate their business, sharpen their mindset, and create lasting impact. Every leader featured in these pages has faced challenges, navigated setbacks, and come out stronger. They've built brands, grown teams, and pushed through self-doubt to create success on their own terms. Their stories aren't just inspiration—they're a blueprint for progress.

Inside, you'll find real strategies—not theory, not fluff, but the exact habits, mindsets, and actions that separate those who struggle from those who thrive. You'll learn how to build influence, overcome rejection, lead with impact, and turn obstacles into leverage. Most importantly, you'll see that success is possible for you, too.

This book is your **mirror**. As you read, you'll recognize your own challenges and ambitions reflected back at you. The question is—will you let them hold you back, or will you use them as fuel to move forward?

The leaders in these pages have already made their choice. Now, it's your turn. This is your playbook. Your wake-up call. Your permission slip to go all in.

The next chapter of your success story starts now.

*"All our dreams can come true,
if we have the courage
to pursue them."*

—Walt Disney

JOHN & KRISTI OAKEY

- Top thirty Power Ranker in the World

- Member of company's Partners Council (Leadership team)

- Six-figure earners

- Convention speakers

- Parents to six kids

Embrace the Suck and Soar: Turning Adversity into Your Advantage

Success isn't something that happens to you—it's something you build. It's forged in the fires of perseverance, grit, and embracing challenges instead of running from them. If you're looking for a shortcut to success, you've come to the wrong place.

Network Marketing isn't about avoiding storms. It's about learning to dance in the rain and thrive despite the chaos. If that sounds tough, that's because it is. But here's the thing: You're tougher.

From Quiet to Chaos: Our Story

To understand the power of perseverance, let me take you back to where our chaos began.

I spent 32+ years in TV news as an anchor, covering everything from breaking news to sports across Texas and Nebraska. My wife Kristi—my high school sweetheart—owns a thriving Home Health Care business. She manages a team, schedules, and the constant demands of a 24/7 operation. Together, we had two boys, and life was already a balancing act.

Then came the moment that changed everything.

As our boys approached adulthood and we prepared to embrace the quieter season of empty nesting, God had other plans. We felt a pull to foster a child. One. Just one daughter to round out our family. But as so often happens, life didn't play by our rulebook. We didn't add just one child—we added four. Three daughters and another son.

Let me set the scene for you. A household that was once on the verge of stillness suddenly became a whirlwind of school schedules, teenage drama, extracurricular activities, and hormonal roller coasters. To top it all off, I was still waking up at 2 a.m. every morning for my news anchor role.

Crazy? Maybe. Exhausting? Absolutely. But those challenges prepared us for what would become our greatest adventure: Network Marketing.

Coach's Note: John and Kristi's decision to embrace chaos rather than shy away from it is the epitome of leadership. Their story proves that success isn't reserved for those with perfect circumstances—it's earned by those who turn obstacles into stepping stones. Reflect on their example: What "chaos" in your life could you embrace and use as fuel for growth? Sometimes the greatest opportunities are disguised as challenges.

The Network Marketing Spark

Despite our full plates, we fell in love with Network Marketing. We loved the products, the mission, and most of all, the idea that we could help others improve their health and their finances. But if you think life paused to make space for this new venture, think again.

What life did, though, was teach us one undeniable truth: Obstacles aren't roadblocks—they're the proving ground for your success. The sooner you learn to embrace the suck, the sooner you can soar.

The 3 C's of Overcoming Obstacles

Success isn't about avoiding challenges; it's about your ability to navigate them. When life knocks you down, these three principles—Calm, Consistency, and Collaboration—will help you get back up stronger.

1. Calm: Expect Disruptions and Plan for Them

The first rule of thriving is understanding that challenges are inevitable. Whether it's a business hiccup, a personal crisis, or a curveball from life, disruptions will happen. But how you react to them is everything.

Actionable Steps:

- Anticipate Chaos: Instead of hoping everything goes perfectly, plan for what could go wrong. Create a "what if" list and pre-plan solutions. For example, if you know a family emergency could derail your work, delegate tasks ahead of time or automate key parts of your business.

- Practice the Pause: In moments of chaos, take a breath before reacting. Give yourself time to assess the situation with a clear head. A calm response leads to better decisions.

- Create Non-Negotiables: No matter how chaotic your day gets, commit to small, daily actions that move your business forward—even if it's just fifteen minutes of focused effort. Consistency compounds.

Coach's Note: The Oakeys' focus on staying calm amidst disruptions is a lesson every entrepreneur can benefit from. Planning ahead for the inevitable bumps in the road isn't just smart—it's essential. Think about your business: Do you have contingency plans in place? Preparation paired with a calm response is the ultimate game-changer, especially when life throws unexpected curveballs.

2. Consistency: Small Steps Lead to Big Wins

It's easy to stay motivated when everything is going well. But the real test is how consistent you can be when the odds are stacked against you. Progress doesn't come from giant leaps—it comes from the small, steady steps you take every single day.

Actionable Steps:

- Simplify Your Routine: Create a checklist of three non-negotiable actions you can take daily for your business, like following up with prospects, posting on social media, or attending team training. Keep it simple but consistent.

- Celebrate Micro-Wins: Don't wait for the big milestones to celebrate. Did you make a call today? Celebrate it. Did you send one message? That's progress. Recognizing small wins builds momentum.

- Fuel Your Mind: Positivity breeds consistency. Start your day with something uplifting—affirmations, a podcast, or even five minutes of gratitude journaling. When your mindset is strong, your actions will follow.

3. Collaboration: Build Your Support Network

One of the biggest lessons we've learned is that you can't—and shouldn't—do this alone. Success in Network Marketing thrives on teamwork. The stronger your support system, the more resilient you'll be when challenges arise.

Actionable Steps:

- Find Your Inner Circle: Surround yourself with people who challenge you to grow and cheer for your wins. This could be your upline, downline, or even a small group of peers outside your business.

- Empower Your Team: Train your team to lead, not just follow. The more independent they are, the more time you'll have to focus on navigating challenges without your business stalling.

- Lean on Mentorship: Don't be afraid to ask for help. Whether it's advice from your upline or insights from a personal mentor, collaboration accelerates growth.

The Emotional Rollercoaster of Network Marketing

There's a moment in every Network Marketer's journey when doubt creeps in. Ours came when our upline left the business during personal struggles. It was a tough blow. We questioned whether we could keep going without that support.

But we didn't quit.

We reminded ourselves why we started. We leaned into the products, the mission, and the lives we'd already impacted. Over time, we found our footing again.

Then, life hit us even harder. Our company underwent three name changes, three ownership transitions, and faced bankruptcy. We lost 75% of our business. For six months, we questioned everything.

Here's what kept us grounded: The products were still great. The compensation plan was still great. The mission was still great.

We decided to stay—and it changed everything. By embracing the new systems, trusting the new ownership, and doubling down on our "why," we had our best year ever.

Embracing the Suck: Your Action Plan

When life feels impossible, remember these steps to help you push through:

1. Reconnect with Your Why: Write down the reason you started. Keep it visible—a sticky note on your desk, a screensaver, or a vision board. Your "why" is your anchor in the storm.

2. Break It Down: When challenges feel overwhelming, simplify. Focus on what you can control today. One message. One call. One step forward.

3. Create Emotional Space: When setbacks happen, give yourself permission to feel frustrated—but don't stay there. Journaling,

talking to a mentor, or even a walk can clear your mind and refocus your energy.

4. Surround Yourself with Resilience: Connect with people who have overcome obstacles in their own journey. Their stories will remind you that setbacks are temporary, but grit lasts forever.

It's Time to Soar

Here's the truth: Life will happen. Challenges will come. But those moments aren't here to break you—they're here to build you.

I'll never forget the day I told Kristi, "Maybe we should just quit." She looked at me, unwavering, and said, "Oakeys don't quit."

So we didn't. We pushed through every storm, every setback, and every doubt. Now, we get to live a life we never imagined possible—a life of impact, freedom, and fulfillment.

This isn't just about business. It's about becoming the person you were meant to be. When you embrace the suck, you'll discover your strength. And when you discover your strength, you'll soar.

So take the first step. Keep moving forward. And remember: You've got what it takes to rise.

Coach's Note: Kristi's simple yet powerful words, "Oakey's don't quit," encapsulate the resilience that drives lasting success. Take this as a challenge: When things get tough, don't just survive—thrive. Create a personal mantra that anchors you during tough times. Like the Oakeys, let it remind you of your strength and your "why" when the temptation to quit arises.

"You can't think and act like a victim and still expect victory"

— Bill Bartmann

RICKY DURANT

- 160 Million Lifetime Team Sales

- 7 Figure Annual Earner

- Qualified 14 leadership retreats

- Earned over 10 company incentive trips

Victim or Victorious: The 5 P's of Network Marketing

Have you ever felt like you're stuck in a cycle where your network marketing efforts seem to lead nowhere? Maybe you're pouring in the hours, yet it feels like you're battling an uphill struggle, facing rejection, and doubting your path. The truth is, as a seasoned network marketing leader earning a seven figure income, a father of two daughters, and husband of twenty three years; I had to learn really fast the difference between being a victim of your circumstances and a victorious leader in network marketing. It is truly an incredible honor to lead and assist the remarkable leadership within my team that have generated over $160 Million in lifetime sales throughout the past eight years since the moment I committed to Network Marketing full time with all I had. What I have discovered is that it often hinges on mastering five critical elements: Sharing your product, building relationships, remaining persistent, finding your passion, and identifying your purpose.

Coach's Note: Ricky's transformation from "ignorance on fire" to a leader who has empowered his team to generate over $160 million in sales is a testament to the power of mindset. If you've ever felt overwhelmed, take this to heart: The choice between being a victim or victorious is made in the moments you decide to keep moving forward, even when it's hard. Reflect on Ricky's story—what's one step you can take today to shift your mindset toward victory?

Network marketing can be a challenging journey, have you ever heard the saying "ignorance on fire" that was me, and I will proudly own it. When I first stepped into this industry, I knew nothing about how compensation plans worked, nothing about how to lead a team, nothing about how to develop leaders, nothing about personal development and probably only ten to twenty friends on social media, but what I did know without a shadow of a doubt is THIS industry could help my family leave the throws of poverty behind. I had the opportunity of a lifetime sitting in the palm of my hands to finally break the chains of generational poverty so that I could provide for my family on an entirely different level, which was MORE than simply financial gain. For years I observed my parents, my grandparents get up and go to work each morning dedicating their life to providing and surviving, but never truly seeing the passion and excitement for all of life's glorious moments. I desired more for my children, my family. I wanted all those moments and let me explain why..... In 2018 when a mass shooter entered the school building in the district where my two daughters attended, taking the lives of thirteen too soon and wounding many, it was like a switch flipped for me. It was a moment of awakening when I realized, God provided me with this beautiful family to love unconditionally, to care for, to provide for, but he never promised me forever and If I didn't get loud and proud with my messaging to impact hundreds of thousands of other families in hopes of allowing them the opportunity to have as many moments and memories as possible with their loved ones without the added stress of past due bills, financial debt interfering in every decision and moment, I was doing a disservice to others, I was guilty of making that decision for them, instead of allowing them to decide for themselves.

Something I know to be fact is Network Marketing is an industry where you can transform obstacles into stepping stones for success, and I want to take this opportunity to share what I have learned along the way, because I know if you're reading this, you can and will make a difference too. Let's first start by focusing on the five P's—Product, People, Persistence, Passion, and Purpose—you can shift from feeling overwhelmed and defeated to becoming empowered and victorious, because let's be honest not every day does everyone "feel" like sunshine and rainbows. This chapter will explore how to effectively implement each of these elements to propel your network marketing business forward.

Coach's Note: Ricky's introduction of the five P's is so simple and yet so profound. Take a moment to assess your own approach to these areas. Are you sharing your product with authenticity? Building relationships with intention? Ricky's persistence and alignment with his purpose helped him overcome personal and professional challenges. Let his story remind you that success is built on consistent small actions in these five areas.

Let's start by introducing you to "Jane", a dedicated network marketer who felt trapped in a constant cycle of rejection and frustration. "Jane" was a passionate individual with a great product but struggled to see the results she hoped for. Every "no" from potential clients and every slow month weighed heavily on her, making her feel like a victim of circumstances beyond her control.

One day, "Jane" decided she had to make a change. She began focusing on mastering the five P's. She worked diligently to improve how she shared her product, developed deeper relationships with people, cultivated persistence, reconnected with her passion, and clarified her purpose. The transformation wasn't instantaneous, but "Jane's" commitment to these principles gradually turned her fortunes around. Her business began to grow, and she moved from feeling like a victim to becoming a victorious network marketer.

"Jane's" story highlights a fundamental point: Success in network marketing is not just about having a great product or working hard; it's about how you approach these five key areas. By embracing the five P's, you can shift from a mindset of defeat to one of victory even if it's been a slower month than what you're accustomed to, transforming your network marketing experience and achieving the success you envision.

Many network marketers struggle with common challenges such as:

- **Sharing the Product:** They often feel pushy or face rejection, which can lead to discouragement.

- **Building Relationships:** They may find it difficult to connect genuinely with others or feel they're not making the right connections, or the judgment they might face.

- **Persistence:** They might struggle to stay motivated during tough times or after repeated setbacks, or when life just gets tough.

- **Finding Passion:** They can lose sight of why they started or feel disheartened when their enthusiasm wanes.

- **Identifying Purpose:** They might not have a clear sense of why their work matters beyond financial gain, leading to burnout or a lack of direction.

These problems can make anyone feel like a victim of their circumstances rather than taking control and steering their own success. Now let's do a deeper dive on how to overcome these common challenges below.

1. PRODUCT: How to Share

- **Mindset Shift:** View sharing your product not as a sales pitch but as a way to offer value. Focus on how your product can solve problems or improve lives.

- **Practice and Preparation:** Develop a clear and concise message about the benefits of your product. Role-play scenarios to build confidence and reduce anxiety.

- **Authenticity:** Share your own experiences with the product. Authenticity helps build trust and makes your message more relatable.

2. PEOPLE: How to Build Relationships

- **Active Listening:** Show genuine interest in others by listening to their needs and concerns. This builds trust and rapport.

- **Follow-Up:** Consistently check in with your contacts, offering support and updates. Building relationships requires ongoing effort.

- **Networking Events:** Attend industry events and engage with potential partners. Networking face-to-face can often lead to stronger connections.

3. PERSISTENT: How to Remain

- **Set Goals:** Establish short-term and long-term goals to keep yourself focused and motivated.

- **Celebrate Small Wins:** Recognize and reward yourself for incremental progress. This keeps you motivated even when big wins seem far off.

- **Develop Resilience:** Understand that setbacks are part of the journey. Learn from them and use them to fuel your determination.

4. PASSION: How to Find

- **Reconnect with Your 'Why':** Reflect on why you started in network marketing. Reconnecting with your initial motivations can reignite your enthusiasm.

- **Seek Inspiration:** Surround yourself with positive influences and successful mentors. Their stories and energy can reignite your own passion.

- **Personal Growth:** Invest in personal development and learning. Growing as an individual can rekindle your passion for business.

5. PURPOSE: How to Identify

- **Define Your Vision:** Clarify what success means to you beyond financial gains. Whether it's helping others, creating a flexible lifestyle, or making an impact, understanding your vision helps keep you focused.

- **Align Actions with Purpose**: Ensure that your daily activities and business strategies align with your purpose. This alignment fosters a sense of fulfillment and direction.

- **Reflect Regularly**: Take time to review and adjust your goals and strategies as needed. Regular reflection helps maintain clarity and ensures you stay on track with your purpose.

As you read through the principles and solutions discussed, ask yourself: *Are you currently feeling like a victim of circumstances like "Jane" in your network marketing journey, or are you ready to step into a victorious mindset?*

Take immediate action by applying the five P's in your network marketing efforts. Start by improving how you share your product, focus on building meaningful relationships, practice persistence, reignite your passion, and clarify your purpose. Remember, the choice between being a victim or victorious is yours. Embrace these strategies and watch as you transform challenges into opportunities for success.

Coach's Note: Ricky's journey is proof that choosing a victorious mindset, coupled with actionable steps, transforms lives. His story about finding his purpose after a life-changing tragedy shows the depth of his "why." As you reflect on this chapter, ask yourself: What's your purpose? Align your daily actions with that vision, and you'll not only overcome challenges but thrive through them.

"If you have a smartphone and you're not making any money from it, it's not very smart is it?"

— Unknown

LEAH LOCKETT

Leah Lockett

- 50k followers across all platforms.

- Corporate real estate background until the age thirty when I found my calling in the NWM industry with a travel based product.

- Sacked my boss fourteen months later after building a six figure income that is now multiple six and on track for seven.

- Has helped thousands of people globally within the industry and trained on stages across the world.

The Velocity Blueprint: Mastering Duplication & Momentum in Network Marketing

Why Duplication is the Heartbeat of Success

In the world of network marketing, success isn't just about how many people you can personally recruit or how many products you can sell. It's about creating a ripple effect—building systems, teams, and leaders who can duplicate your success without your constant hand-holding. This chapter is designed to help you master the art of duplication and create unstoppable momentum within your network marketing business.

If you're reading this, you're likely already driven. You've got ambition, perhaps even a taste of success. But now you want velocity— growth that compounds, a team that thrives with or without you, and a business that feels more like freedom than a full-time job.

Coach's Notes - *Pay close attention. Leah has that incredible ambitious energy. She is a mover and shaker always taking action. I am impressed at how she is always at the cutting edge of the best strategies. She invests constantly in herself, takes action and then shares her insights. She has broken down a complex concept in a very simple way!*

Let's dive into the strategies that will transform your approach to network marketing, turning you from a recruiter into a leader who inspires duplication and sustainable growth.

1. The Fundamentals of Network Marketing: Simplicity Over Complexity

While many overcomplicate network marketing, the truth is simple: success is built on a foundation of basic activities, done consistently and taught effectively. The fundamentals are not glamorous, but they are powerful when executed with precision.

- Know What Moves the Needle: Income-Producing Activities (IPAs) are your bread and butter. These include prospecting, presenting, following up, and closing. Master these, teach these, and your business grows.

- Documentation Isn't Magic: Leaders with impressive results didn't stumble upon secret hacks. They simply did the basics consistently over time and taught others to do the same.

- The Power of Teaching: It's not enough to know what to do—you must teach it. Use the "Teach, Show, Go" model:

  - Teach the process.

  - Show it in action.

  - Then let your team Go execute while you support them.

Key Takeaway: The learning is in the doing, not the watching. People don't duplicate what you say—they duplicate what you do.

2. The Posture Problem: Confidence is the Currency of Influence

Posture in network marketing isn't about arrogance; it's about unwavering belief in what you offer, regardless of external opinions. Without posture, you'll find yourself chasing prospects, craving validation, and burning out.

- Posture Defined: It's the belief in your opportunity, products, and yourself, even when faced with rejection or scepticism.

- Why It Matters: Prospects can sense uncertainty. When your confidence wavers, they feel it, and it erodes their interest. But when you stand firm in your belief, they're more likely to trust you—even if they don't fully understand the business yet.

- Sorting, Not Convincing: Professional network marketers don't convince people to join. They sort through prospects to find those already looking for an opportunity. Your job isn't to make someone see the value; it's to identify who's ready to receive it.

Pro Tip: The moment you stop caring whether someone says yes or no—and start focusing on finding the right fit—you gain the posture that attracts success.

Coach's Notes - *Leah nailed it. Oftentimes in network marketing we are so worried about what others think we shy away from showing any confidence. Posture up! Enthusiasm and posture sell. No one wants to follow or buy from someone who shows zero confidence.*

3. Speaking to the Right Prospects: The Color Code Approach

Not all prospects are created equal. Understanding how to identify and communicate with different types of people increases your effectiveness and duplication potential.

- Red Prospects (Leaders): These are high-achievers—people you look up to. They're often the hardest to recruit because they don't need you. Approach them with respect, focusing on how the opportunity aligns with their goals, not yours.

- Blue Prospects (Seekers): These individuals look up to you. They're the easiest to recruit because they're already inspired by your success. Highlight how you've solved the very problems they're facing.

- Green Prospects (Peers): These are your equals—friends, colleagues,
- people in your current network. They're often sceptical but open-minded.
- Connect through shared experiences and common challenges.

Communication Tip: Adjust your approach based on the prospect's mindset, not your script. Flexibility is the key to influence.

4. Recruiting Through, Not Just To

Most network marketers make the mistake of focusing solely on recruiting individuals. The real magic happens when you recruit through people—leveraging their networks to create exponential growth.

- The Shift in Perspective: Recruiting to someone means you're fixated on that one person joining. Recruiting through someone means you see them as a gateway to an entire network of potential leaders and customers.

- The Domino Effect: When you bring in one new person, don't stop there. Ask, "Who do you know that would benefit from this opportunity?" Your newest recruit is often the bridge to prospects you would've never met otherwise.

- Duplication in Action: Teach your team to recruit through their warm markets immediately. This creates layers of growth, reducing dependency on any single individual.

5. The Science of Duplication: Creating Systems, Not Stars

Duplication is the key to sustainability. Without it, you're a one-person show—a "one-man band," hustling to keep the music playing. With it, you create leverage, scalability, and freedom.

- Why Duplication Matters: It's not just about your income. It's about creating success in others, which in turn secures your own.

- Success Loves Speed: People lose excitement if they don't see quick wins. Create simple, fast-start systems that help new team members experience success early.

Golden Rule: If it's not simple, it won't duplicate. If it requires your constant involvement, it's not a system.

Coach's Notes - *One of my favorite quotes is from Leonardo DaVinci is "Simplicity is the ultimate sophistication." Sometimes systems are so good they actually suck! Why? Because they are complicated. What works is what duplicates.*

6. Building with Intention: Leadership is a Choice, Not a Title

You can't accidentally become a great leader. It requires intention, self-awareness, and a commitment to growth—not just for yourself but for your team.

• Shift Your Focus: Stop thinking about what the business can do for you and start focusing on what it can do for others. Your success is a by-product of the value you create.

• Lead with Residual Impact: Don't just chase residual income—create residual impact. Teach people how to fish, and they'll feed themselves (and others) for a lifetime.

• Model the Mindset: The way you think becomes the way your team thinks. If you're obsessed with growth, learning, and leadership, they will be too.

7. Becoming a Student of the Profession: The Path to Mastery

The best leaders are lifelong students. In network marketing, you don't graduate from learning—you evolve through it.

- Educate to Elevate: The more you understand about the industry, the easier it is to inspire others. Knowledge builds confidence, and confidence builds leaders.

- Manage Expectations: Network marketing isn't a get-rich-quick scheme. It's a business. Set long-term goals, focus on daily actions, and teach your team to do the same.

- Normalise Excellence: Your job as a leader isn't just to hit your goals—it's to raise the standard. Make success the norm in your organization, not the exception.

Final Thoughts: The Momentum Multiplier

Momentum isn't a mystery. It's the natural result of consistent action, effective duplication, and inspired leadership. When you combine these elements, you create a business that grows with or without you—a business rooted in systems, not personalities.

Remember:

- You don't need to be the smartest, most charismatic, or most experienced person in the room. You just need to be the one who shows up, stays consistent, and teaches others to do the same.

- Duplication is the heartbeat of network marketing. Master it, and you'll create not just income, but impact—the kind that changes lives, starting with your own.

Now go out there and build with velocity.

Action Step: Reflect on your current business. Are you focusing on activities that duplicate? Are you recruiting through people or just to them? Identify one area where you can simplify, systematise, or shift your mindset—and take action today.

"You can't fight the waves, but you can learn how to surf."

– Jon Kabat

AMBER GUSTOWSKI

- Ten years in NWM profession

- Heart led seven-figure earner

- Top 1% of the company

- Top three company earner

- Helped create thousands of 4 and 5 figure earners

Building Through Adversity and Adjusting Your Crown

What if I told you that your most painful challenges could be the key to actually unlocking your greatest power? I know you're probably sitting there and just rolled your eyes, I did too when I'd read truth-bombs like this, especially when I was in the thick of it. I'd think to myself "So you're saying that the adversity I'm facing isn't here to break me—but to BUILD me?!" I didn't want to believe this, I'd rather stay cozy in my pity party blanket fort. I spent years doubting myself, my worth, and whether I even had what it took to succeed in life, let alone network marketing! But as I look back now, I realize that everything I went through was preparing me for this beautiful journey of abundance, and I know in my heart it's possible for you too.

Coach's Note: Amber's story shows that challenges aren't barriers—they're bridges. Use your hardships as stepping stones to build the life you've always envisioned.

Let's be honest, we all go through seasons of hardship and life definitely doesn't stop when you start building your business; if anything it tests you even more! To this day I am still juggling this, but one thing I've learned over the years is that you can't fight the waves but you can learn how to surf, and in the end that brings me so much peace every single time. I get it, the pressure of running a network marketing business while balancing family, bills, and your personal life can feel more like walking through fire. I truly believe it's in that fire that you are forged into the leader you're meant to be, and then you're truly unstoppable!

I wasn't born with a silver spoon, nor was I raised in an environment that encouraged me to dream big. In fact, I was born into child and family services with my fifteen year old Mom, living in over thirty seven homes and enduring a childhood of confusion, emotional and mental abuse that left me questioning whether I was ever enough, or if I'd ever feel safe or truly loved. Did I even trust myself?

Those scars stayed with me for years, they still creep up. They made me believe that success was for other people—people who had better upbringings, who were smarter, wealthier, or more capable than me. I didn't realize how much shame I felt just for being ME. I carried that belief into my adulthood and I didn't really have big dreams because I was too busy living in survival mode.

I was a young mom who was waitressing long nights just to scrape by, my husband was working overtime and we rarely saw each other with our schedules. I was exhausted, depressed, full of Mom guilt and our marriage was hurting. The weight of our financial struggles felt like this huge anchor pulling me down and I felt so unsafe. Despite this, I was determined to be the best Mom and woman I could be for my three babies; I desperately wanted to give them a life of security, blessings and possibility. I wanted to be an example of a powerful and loving woman to my daughter, to show her mountains can be moved and she can too! It was in those 3AM moments, lying in bed wide awake, heart pounding when I knew something had to change. I was determined to go from broke(n) to blessed, and from burnt out to burning bright! It was in those moments where I found my "why" and the strength to get through anything and it burned deep in my heart. There was a light inside me, I just needed the courage to turn it on.

In the middle of this crazy storm is actually when I found network marketing— I immediately saw possibility and it gave me hope and butterflies in my tummy. You mean I can stay home with my kids wearing my leggings and slippers and make money?! As in, uncapped earning potential?! Did you just say residual income?? You mean I can actually start to feel better and help other people too?! I was all in, and so I became a student in my first company and earned while I learned, It was pretty cool.

Family and friends doubted and questioned me, but I quickly learned they weren't the ones paying my bills, fixing my credit score, or giving me more quality time and experiences with my three babies and husband. I learned that people will talk behind your back no matter how kind or successful you are, it's always a sting to the heart but there's a reason why they are behind you and you deserve to stay laser focussed! Trust me, it's all worth it for the peace of mind, quality time with your loved ones, financial freedom, time freedom, and a chance to rewrite your story.

Believe me when I say that this now confident, seven figure earner who sits at the top 1% of her company's transformation didn't come instantly or easily. I played this "pity party adversity game" for over eight years in my Network Marketing career, and that was way too long! Although I was strong and had great leadership skills, built big teams and was great with people, when tough times came I really struggled. I learned a ton, I made money and memories, and there were also inevitable failures, pivots and changes along the way that would set me back way more than I should have let them. But what I had that set me apart from the 99%, was a deep hunger to make this profession work, that burnt deep within my heart. In the end what it really came down to was relentless, confident, postured action day in and day out, topped with relentless belief in myself and what I had in my hands. My mindset was everything, the victim blame game mentality had to go. I did this day in and day out, and I started to see the light. In those moments of doubt, stress, and even failure, I found my power, it was hiding deep in my belly and it burned in my heart...I knew I just had to trust and keep taking action. I actually remember looking at myself in the mirror three years ago and saying out loud like a crazy person "Amber, you are where you ARE and are NOT in your life because of you...Nobody else. Are you finally going to start playing big?! You know what to do." In that moment of full accountability with myself the game changed...I changed. I discovered that adversity isn't something to fear—it's something to embrace. It's what allows you to stand tall in the face of anything that comes your way in your network marketing business, and to keep moving forward, because you're worth it.

Coach's Note: Accountability is the ultimate difference maker. When you take ownership of your results, you reclaim your power to create the future you desire.

So, if you don't already know, adversity is a given...but so is finding your power. Whether it's in your business, personal struggles, financial difficulties, or doubts from those around you, you'll face hard times. But it's in those moments where you have the opportunity to rise up and remember who you are! Remember why you are doing this and turn your light all the way up! I started to change all my WTF (what the fudge) thoughts into WIT (whatever it takes) thoughts and everything started to shift. It felt lighter, more empowering. Try it!

In my one on one coaching sessions, one of the most common things that come up is self-doubt and a poor mindset. It's easy to feel overwhelmed when the obstacles stack up—when you're juggling a million responsibilities, facing rejection, or dealing with personal issues. These moments can make you question everything: Is this worth it? Do I have what it takes? Why is this so hard? It's a terrible feeling! In those dark moments, it's easy to let fear win and to let it convince you that you're not enough, but the truth is adversity is only as powerful as the story you tell yourself about it. Remember, it's not here to BREAK you, but to BUILD you and you are simply learning how to surf the waves! Every time a negative story creeps up, I simply say out loud "clear, cancel, delete" and I choose the next highest thought. It works every time.

I want to give you some of my superpowers that I've found over the years that help me build my network marketing business through the hard times. They help me readjust my crown, find my personal power, and push through when it feels impossible:

1. Remember who you are deep in your heart. If your intentions are good and your heart is pure, you'll find your way.

2. Your "why" is the anchor that will keep you grounded when the storms hit. Let your "why" give you a burn deep within your

beautiful soul. On days when I didn't want to show up, I reminded myself why I started. You need to do the same. Write down your why. Visualize it. Let it fuel you when the road gets rough.

3. Tap into your personal power. Adversity has a way of clouding your vision and making you forget who we really are. You are powerful. You are worthy of success. You are unbreakable! Don't let fear and doubt rob you of your potential. Every challenge you face is an opportunity to tap into your strength and prove to yourself what you're capable of. Adjust your crown and keep moving!

4. Give yourself grace, and don't give up. Take accountability, then turn your self loathing into self love and self belief! There will be days when it feels like everything and everyone is against you. In those moments, give yourself grace. It's okay to feel overwhelmed. It's okay to struggle. But don't let that be the reason you quit. Keep moving forward, even if it's just one small step at a time.

5. You can't fight the waves but you can learn how to surf. After a while it gets easier and easier, and before you know it even the big waves don't frighten you, instead they excite you.

6. Turn your WTF (what the fudge) moments into WIT (whatever it takes) moments...Start doing this and your game will change.

7. Clear, Cancel, Delete...Choose the next highest thought.

8. Trust the process while taking relentless action.

Coach's Note: Adversity reveals your inner strength. Amber's practical tips are more than strategies; they're lifelines to keep you grounded and growing through life's toughest seasons. I have the opportunity to personally work with Amber and watch her consistently crush her business.

In the end, I hope the thought of building through adversity no longer makes you want to crawl into the fetal position and hide in your blanket for drinking slurpees (can you tell I'm Canadian) for seven days straight. It is simply a part of life, and it doesn't have to completely define you. Instead, let it be your guiding light. Let it be the thing that builds you into the leader, the entrepreneur, the parent and the person you're meant to be. When you face challenges, remind yourself of your why, tap into your power, adjust your crown and keep pushing forward.

You have the power within you to build a life of freedom, abundance, and purpose. None of this is negotiable or up for debate. I know this because I've lived it. I can be unstoppable, so can you.

JENNIFER (JENN) GLACKEN

- 30 years in the Network Marketing Industry, all with one company

- Multiple Six-Figure Earner

- Creator of the Social Media Champion's Blueprint

- Featured in Hal Elrod's book "Miracle Morning for Network Marketers"

Developing Resilience: Running Through the Finish Line

After years of longing and waiting, a couple's dream finally came true—a baby girl was born. But that joy quickly turned into a heart-wrenching challenge. Their daughter was born with her legs backward. Faced with a tough decision, they chose to have the doctor break and reset her tiny legs, leaving her in casts and braces for the first eighteen months of her life. When the braces finally came off, her journey wasn't over. To help her legs develop correctly, the doctor recommended putting her shoes on the wrong feet, making the daunting task of learning to walk even harder.

Determined to help their daughter gain strength, her parents enrolled her in ballet classes. But for this little girl, every plié came with pain. After a few months, she quit—it was just too much.

Years later, something changed. That same little girl fell in love with ballet. She decided she wanted to be a ballerina—a dream that surprised everyone. Her legs didn't work like other kids, and even the simplest steps were a struggle. But this time, she refused to quit. She embraced the pain, the hard work, and the setbacks, holding tightly to her vision of dancing on stage.

And she did it. Through grit and determination, she eventually became a professional ballerina. **That little girl was me.**

Coach's Note: Jenn's story is a powerful reminder that success is built on resilience, not just talent or opportunity. She could have let the pain define her, but instead, she let it refine her. How many of us quit before we even give ourselves a real shot? Success isn't about avoiding hardship—it's about pushing through it.

Ballet was my first introduction to resilience, and it shaped how I approach challenges to this day. Working through physical limitations tested not just my body, but my mind. I had to find ways to work with what I had, and learned that even the hardest obstacles could be overcome with persistence and creativity.

Though my path eventually shifted from ballet to college, marriage, motherhood, and building a network marketing business, the lessons I learned remain the same.

In network marketing, the challenges may look different, but the principles of resilience are universal. Life will throw curveballs—it's inevitable. Whether it's a slow month, distributors quitting, or customers returning products, resilience is what keeps you moving forward. The same drive that took me from braces and casts to a stage as a ballerina is the same drive that fuels success in business and life.

Resilience comes from determination to learn from challenges and push forward until a solution is found. In network marketing, that means remembering that setbacks are just stepping stones on the path to success.

What does it take to bounce back after a disappointment and keep going when the odds are stacked against you? How do you teach your team to do the same? Building that inner toughness isn't just a skill; it's the backbone of success in network marketing—and life. Without it, even the most talented individuals give up before they ever reach their full potential.

How do you build this critical skill and why is it essential to "run to and through the finish line?"

Resilience: Deciding Not to Give Up

Resilience is born the moment you decide not to give up. It's not about avoiding challenges—it's about how you respond when they come your way. Life will always present obstacles, but resilience is the ability to adapt, persist, and even thrive in the face of adversity.

In network marketing, challenges come in many forms: a slow month, a missed goal, or a top leader leaving. The temptation to throw in the towel can be strong, but it's in these moments that resilience is forged.

When times are tough, pushing through them and continuing to run towards the goal builds an inner toughness, something no one is born with. You only build it through experience.

Each obstacle, failure, or disappointment is an opportunity to strengthen your resilience. Think of it like a muscle: the more you work it, the stronger it becomes. It's not just about enduring tough times; it's about using those experiences to grow and learn.

Viktor Frankl, a psychiatrist, and Holocaust survivor, endured the unimaginable horrors of Nazi concentration camps. Despite the suffering, Frankl discovered that resilience comes from finding meaning in adversity. He observed that those who survived often had a purpose— something greater to live for. For Frankl, it was the hope of completing his life's work and helping others. His groundbreaking philosophy, shared in *Man's Search for Meaning*, emphasizes that while we cannot always control our circumstances, we can always choose our response, transforming even the deepest suffering into strength and purpose.

Coach's Note: The best network marketers aren't the ones who never struggle—they're the ones who refuse to stay down. Jenn's story and Frankl's philosophy highlight the same truth: you can either let adversity break you or build you. The choice is yours. If you truly want success, decide that quitting is not an option.

This reminds us that resilience is a choice—a mindset. It's not about the size of the challenge but about the size of your determination to overcome it. Whether you're facing a business hurdle or a personal struggle, the decision to keep going builds that inner fortitude.

To develop this kind of resilience, here are some things I've learned to do:

1. **Decide that quitting is not an option.** Once you commit to this mindset, every setback becomes a stepping stone rather than a stopping point. "Success is the only option" must be the mentality.

2. **Learn to laugh at yourself.** Humor can help you get through even some of the toughest times.

3. **Focus on the "why," not just the "how."** Keep the big picture in mind—what are you running toward? Your goal must be stronger than your obstacles.

4. **Be flexible and nimble.** Things change all the time. Developing the skill to remain flexible will serve you well in network marketing and life.

5. **Take small, consistent actions.** Keep trying despite the difficulty. Even when you don't feel motivated, discipline and perseverance will carry you through.

Resilience begins with a single decision: deciding to run to and through a goal 100%. Quitting is not an option.

Resilience Starts with Awareness

Social media has changed network marketing. The pace of change continues to quicken making it challenging for many in our industry to keep up; especially if they built their business years ago.

I've been a top leader in network marketing for 30+ years and built the "old school" way: hosting in-home events, talking to strangers, and making a list of 100 names. These methods worked at the time.

In 2021, my team was asking how to build online and, frankly, I didn't know what to teach them to do. I invested in mentorship to learn how to build online. Now, my team has modern, digital systems that work. But, this took awareness.

Awareness that:

1. I didn't know how to build online

2. I needed to invest in mentorship to learn

I developed a new muscle, learned new skills and figured out what works, what doesn't work and what needs to be tweaked.

Before building resilience, we need to understand where we stand. Think of it like a GPS—if you don't know your current location, it's hard to map out a route to your destination. Resilience begins with self-awareness. Where are you in relation to your goal? Be honest with yourself.

Once you've taken stock of where you stand, the next step is to take intentional action. Rome wasn't built overnight—it's a process of small, consistent changes that add up over time.

Run to and Through the Finish Line

In network marketing, success often comes to those who push through the hardest moments. Too many people stop short of their goals, sometimes because they lack skills and sometimes because they lack perseverance.

I've had team members who embodied resilience by running to and through the finish line. One of them, Theresa, had an opportunity to qualify for her first incentive trip. With just a few weeks left, she needed to achieve 13,000 in sales volume—more than she had ever done in a single month. This same month, her mom had a health scare which could have derailed Theresa.

But it didn't. She spent hours at the hospital with her mom *and* figured out how to get her volume. Her volume grew, her organization grew and she grew personally. Theresa leaned into the challenge, strategized her time, and gave her all. In the end, she not only hit her goal but also proved to herself that she could handle anything life threw her way.

Resilience is built in these critical moments when you choose to finish strong. The act of completing your goal—even if it's not perfect—builds belief in yourself and inspires others to do the same.

Coach's Note: There's something about pushing through when you feel like stopping that changes you. Theresa's story is proof that the real transformation isn't just about hitting a goal—it's about who you become in the process. Success isn't just about achieving something; it's about developing the grit to fight through resistance and finish what you start.

To foster a mindset of running to and through the finish line:

1. **Set clear goals with checkpoints.** Break your goal into smaller chunks to create momentum. Start with the end and work your way backward to break the goal into smaller, manageable milestones.

2. **Celebrate progress**, not just results. Small wins fuel big achievements. Have small rewards along the way. This adds fun to the adventure and honors the hard work you're putting in.

3. **Visualize the finish line.** Imagine how it will feel when you cross it. Let that vision pull you forward. Allow yourself time every day to think about where you are going. Those with a strong vision work harder to achieve it.

Don't stop halfway, convinced it's impossible to finish. That's giving up without even trying. Train yourself and your team to always run to the finish line, no matter how far away it seems.

Learning from Mistakes and Setbacks

Mistakes and setbacks are inevitable in life and business, but how you respond to them shapes your path forward. Resilient leaders don't let obstacles define them—they let obstacles refine them.

Years ago, I traveled to California to support a new distributor. The trip was meticulously planned—flights booked, hotels reserved, and an agenda confirmed with the distributor. Everything seemed to be set. But upon arrival, things took an unexpected turn. I showed up at the distributor's home for an evening meeting, only to be met with silence. No one answered the door. No one opened the curtains. Calls to the distributor went unanswered. It was a complete "no-show" event.

Though the experience was frustrating and costly, it taught me a valuable lesson. It taught me to reflect on what worked—I showed up prepared. What didn't work—the distributor was unresponsive. And what needed to change—I needed a system for qualifying when to invest in traveling to support new teammates. Resilience was built by learning from the situation and adjusting for the future.

Resilient leaders look for the lessons in their mistakes to avoid repeating them.

When facing adversity, focus on what you can control and how you can make a difference. The one thing you always have power over is your mindset. Leading with a resourceful mindset not only strengthens your own resilience but also inspires your team to adopt the same approach.

No matter what happens—whether it's a success or a setback—stay in a state of evaluation, not judgment. Ask yourself these three questions:

1. **What worked?**

2. **What didn't work?**

3. **What can I tweak for next time?**

By asking these questions, you shift from frustration to growth, allowing setbacks to become stepping stones for future success. This habit of reflection and adjustment is a cornerstone of resilience and will serve you well in your journey as a leader.

Resilience is Your Superpower

Resilience is the thread that ties everything together in network marketing. It's what keeps you going when others quit, what pushes you to hit that final goal, and what inspires your team to rise with you.

Whether you're facing a personal challenge, like I did with my legs, or pushing toward a business milestone, remember this: resilience isn't about avoiding adversity—it's about what you do when it shows up.

Decide today to become resilient. Run to and through every finish line. Build a culture of perseverance within your team. Then, watch as your belief, confidence, and success soar.

"If you are not willing to learn, no one can help you, but if you are willing to learn, no one can stop you!"

– Marc Accetta

SHELLY TAYLOR

- Director Developer award

- Mover and Shaker award

- Dream Trip winner to Punta Cana

Early in 2022, I found myself racing against the clock again, juggling the demands of being a hairstylist, a fitness instructor, and most importantly, a wife and mom to two incredible boys. One night, I was driving back to the salon for a late client. My husband and our two sons were on their way to basketball games—my youngest was in his first year of sixth-grade basketball, and my oldest was being coached by my husband on his ninth-grade team.

As I drove, the familiar ache of missing another family moment settled in. I loved my work as a hairstylist, but the late nights, weekends, and even holidays had become all too normal. Inflation had hit hard, and while the extra money helped us cover Christmas and other expenses, it came at a steep cost: my time with my family. I remember gripping the steering wheel and crying out to God, *There has to be something more. There has to be a way to provide for my family without missing out on their lives.*

Little did I know, God was already setting things in motion.

Coach's Note: Shelly's story is one that so many people can relate to—being stretched thin while searching for something *more*. What's powerful here is that she didn't just wait for the perfect opportunity to show up—she was open to new possibilities, even when she didn't see them right away. Sometimes, the answers to our biggest prayers are hidden in places we least expect.

A New Opportunity

A few months later, a friend reached out to me about a new health and wellness company she had partnered with. She was excited, passionate, and eager to share the opportunity with me. I listened, but I wasn't interested. I was already happy with the supplements I was taking. Not only am I a hairstylist, but also a fitness instructor, and I had no intention of adding "salesperson" to my already packed schedule, but my friend was persistent. She kept reaching out, sharing updates about the company and the products. I admired her dedication, but I kept saying no. Then one day, curiosity got the better of me. I read the ingredients in the products she was promoting, and to my surprise, I was impressed. They were clean, effective, and aligned with my fitness philosophy.

At that moment, I realized I wanted to try the products—not to sell them, but for my own health and wellness. Like many others, I wanted the best price possible. Reluctantly, I signed up as a brand partner, adamant that I was only in it for the discount. I told myself, *I'm not selling anything. I'm just a customer.*

From Hesitant to Hopeful

What happened next surprised me. Without even trying, my business started to grow. People noticed a difference in my energy, my enthusiasm, and my results. Friends, family, and even clients began asking questions. They wanted to know what I was doing and how they could get started too.

Before I knew it, I was sharing my story—authentically and naturally. It didn't feel like "selling" because I was simply talking about something I genuinely loved. The more I shared, the more I realized how much this business could impact our lives.

Then came the talk of attending conference. It was the company's annual event, and everyone was buzzing about it. The only problem? It was in Florida, and we lived in Texas. My husband and I hadn't flown in thirteen years. Over time, we had developed a fear of flying, and the idea of leaving our kids behind terrified me.

At first, I dismissed the idea altogether. But one of my leaders reached out with a simple message: "Shelly, I see you." Those four words stirred something deep inside me. Someone believed in me—saw my potential—even when I couldn't fully see it myself. After praying and discussing it with my husband, we decided to go. It was a leap of faith, both literally and figuratively.

Coach's Note: This is such a pivotal moment in Shelly's journey. Sometimes, all it takes is one person speaking life into you for you to step into your potential. If you've ever had someone believe in you before you believed in yourself—*you know how powerful that is*. And if you *haven't* had that person yet—let me tell you, you are capable of more than you realize.

The Turning Point

That conference changed everything. Walking into the event, I felt the energy and excitement radiating from every corner. The stories I heard, the people I met, and the lessons I learned lit a fire in me that I hadn't felt in years. For the first time, I saw this business as more than just a side hustle. It was a vehicle for personal growth, financial freedom, and most importantly, the time freedom I had been praying for.

God was answering my prayers in ways I never expected. He wasn't just providing a way to make extra money—He was opening doors to opportunities that allowed me to grow as a person, overcome my fears, and create a life I had only dreamed of.

Lessons Learned

Two years later, I'm still on this journey. I'm still learning, still growing, and still praying. But along the way, I've discovered some invaluable lessons that have helped me build a thriving network marketing business.

1. Get Into Action

The first and most important lesson I've learned is the power of action. When I first started, I was hesitant to tell people about my business. I didn't want to come across as pushy or salesy. But I quickly realized that if I wanted to succeed, I needed to share my story authentically.

For me, that meant telling my friends and family about my business and why I was passionate about it. It also meant showing up consistently on social media. I started posting daily—sharing not just about my business, but about my life. I made reels, went live, and stayed true to who I am.

Authenticity has been my guiding principle. Staying in action is easy during the busy seasons when momentum is high, but it's crucial to continue during the slower seasons too. Consistency builds trust and keeps the business growing.

2. Stay Close to the Fire (Go to Company Events)

Another lesson I've learned is the importance of staying connected. Whether it's jumping on team calls, attending local events, or traveling to corporate conferences, staying close to the fire keeps me motivated and inspired.

Smaller local events are great for building relationships and keeping the excitement alive. I've hosted gatherings at my house, met with team members at local restaurants, and made it a priority to stay engaged with my community. But it's the corporate events that fuel my vision.

3. Set a Clear Vision

The most valuable lesson I've learned is the importance of vision and goal-setting. Without a clear vision, it's easy to lose focus or get discouraged. I've learned to write down my goals—both short-term and long-term—and keep them in front of me every day.

This business has allowed me to dream bigger than I ever imagined. Because of it, I've been asked to speak on stage at corporate events and regional meetings. I've won the Director Developer award, Mover and Shaker award, and achieved milestones in personal sales and team building that I never thought possible. One of the most exciting blessings was earning a dream trip to Punta Cana in the Dominican Republic—a moment that felt like God's tangible confirmation that I was on the right path.

Knowing what I want and why I want it gives me the drive to keep going, even on the days when I don't feel like working. Discipline, not motivation is what keeps me moving forward.

4. Personal Development

Personal development is key to success in Network Marketing. By improving our mindset, communication, and leadership, we build stronger connections and inspire growth. Success isn't just about selling—it's about becoming the best version of ourselves to add value and create lasting impact.

Coach's Note: Success leaves clues, and Shelly just laid out a roadmap for anyone looking to build something meaningful. Take action, stay plugged in, set a clear vision, and invest in personal growth. These aren't just tips for business—they are principles for life.

The Answer to My Prayers

Looking back, I can see how every step of this journey has been part of God's plan. From the late nights at the salon to the hesitant "yes" to network marketing, every moment has led me to where I am today.

This business has provided for my family in ways I never imagined. It's given us financial freedom, time freedom, and the ability to dream again. More importantly, it's allowed me to be there for my boys—to cheer them on at their games, celebrate their milestones, and create memories that will last a lifetime.

I'm not yet where I want to be, but I know I'm on the right path. God is still answering prayers, opening doors, and teaching me lessons along the way. And for that, I am forever grateful.

A Message to You

If you're reading this and wondering if network marketing could be the answer to your prayers, I encourage you to take a leap of faith. You don't have to have all the answers or know all the steps. Just start.

Share your story. Stay close to the fire. Set a clear vision. Most importantly, trust that God is working behind the scenes, opening doors you never knew existed.

Success starts with consistent action—don't wait, take the first step today. Surround yourself with energy and inspiration by staying connected and attending events. Keep your focus sharp by envisioning your goals clearly and working toward them daily. Most importantly, invest in personal growth to unlock your full potential and lead with confidence.

Answered prayers don't always look the way we expect them to. But when you step out in faith and trust the process, you'll find that God's plan is always greater than your own. Take that step—you just might find your own "answered prayers" waiting on the other side.

"Do not judge me by my success, judge me by how many times I fell down and got back up again."

— Nelson Mandela

CORRINA D'ALESSIO

- Life & Performance Coach

- Multiple 6+ Figure Earner in 4 years

- Holistic Nutritional Coach

- Corporate Communication Facilitator

Resilient by Design – How I Became Unbreakable

What if the very obstacles meant to break you became the foundation of your unbreakable spirit?

"In the midst of winter, I found there was, within me, an invincible summer."

– Albert Camus

Some lives may seem ordinary from the outside, but within them lies a tapestry of strength woven from challenge after challenge. Mine is one of those lives. Raised by a single mother, my story began with lessons in resilience from a woman who faced her own struggles while raising two daughters. My parents divorced when I was just two years old. Sundays were my time with my dad, but my primary home—my foundation—was with my mom.

My Mom and I lived together for many years until she started dating someone seriously, and at the age of 12, my sister was born. It was an unexpected and joyful addition, but it highlighted my mom's strength as she navigated raising two girls in a world that demanded so much of her. Without realizing it, I was learning to face challenges with courage, grit, and determination—lessons that would serve me well when my life became turbulent.

At 16, life handed me my first true test. After recovering from a major leg operation, I discovered I was five months pregnant. Shock, confusion, and fear hit me like a tidal wave. I was still a child, trying to figure out my place in the world, and now I had a life-altering decision. I traveled from Canada to the U.S. to give the baby up for adoption. It was the most heart-wrenching choice I have ever made, one that left me questioning everything about myself. But even in the pain, I found my strength—the ability to make decisions not for myself, but for the betterment of another life. At this time in my life, I was broken. I made one bad decision after another and that carried on for several years.

Coach's Note: Corrina's story is a perfect example of what it means to be battle-tested. Every challenge she faced could have been a reason to stop. Instead, she used them as a reason to push forward. The strongest leaders aren't the ones who had it easy—they're the

ones who learned how to get back up every time life knocked them down.

Only two and a half years later, I was pregnant again. This time, I knew I couldn't give up my child. I chose to raise my son, even though I understood the challenges ahead. The relationship with his father couldn't withstand the life pressures and we went our separate ways. But through it all, my son became my anchor, my reason to persevere. He taught me to think of others, work hard, strive for more, give more. We grew up together and still, to this very day, have an unbreakable bond.

For many years, I was a single mom. My world revolved around my son, and I poured every ounce of energy into ensuring he felt safe, loved, and supported. Life wasn't easy, I worked two jobs and went to college, but I was determined to show him that obstacles weren't the end of the road—they were growth opportunities. Whether I was juggling two jobs or navigating the emotional weight of parenting alone, I wanted my son to see that resilience is not about avoiding hardship, but about rising in the face of it.

A few years later, I entered a six-year relationship that led to marriage and shortly after, my daughter was born. She brought so much light into my life, but the marriage wasn't built to last. By the time she was two, we had split. Once again, I found myself a single mom, balancing the needs of now two children while figuring out how to rebuild my life, after leaving with nothing.

Seems as though I was creating a pattern of choosing the hard road. I got remarried, thinking I had found a fresh start. Instead, I found myself in a tumultuous relationship with a man who struggled with depression and anxiety. The darkness of that time tested me in ways I could never have anticipated. I was carrying the emotional weight of the relationship while trying to maintain a sense of stability for my children.

But it was during that relationship that I discovered a new path—one I didn't expect. I found Network Marketing. What began as a way to make ends meet soon became so much more. Network Marketing wasn't just a career; it became a lifeline, a platform for growth, and a source of strength. It taught me how to lead, how to inspire, how to solve problems, and most importantly to believe in myself and my worth. For the first six years, success seems elusive. However, the past four years have been transformative. I had to embrace the belief that I could succeed here. I choose to go all in, stop playing small, and give in to the system. I made more than $100k my first year and helped a few others do the same.

Coach's Note: What changed? Corrina made a decision. The moment she stopped doubting herself and played full out, everything shifted. Most people in this industry wait for confidence before they take action. The truth? Confidence comes FROM taking action. Stop waiting and start doing.

As I built my business, I remained steadfast in my commitment to my children. They were always my priority, my "why." Every decision I made, every late night I worked, and there were many, every obstacle I faced, was with them in mind. I wanted them to see firsthand what resilience looked like. I wanted them to know that no matter how many times life knocked me down, I would always rise—and so could they.

The last couple of years have brought challenges I could never have imagined. Reflecting on my journey, I recognize that resilience has been my guiding force. The challenges of early motherhood, failed marriages, and career uncertainties could have led to despair. Instead, they became catalysts for growth, teaching me that resilience is not about avoiding hardships but confronting and transforming them. You have to decide that no matter how hard things get, you won't quit.

Instead of focusing on the problem, I turned my attention to the solution. I asked myself, *"What can I do right now to create a different outcome?"* For me, that meant leaning into my Network Marketing business. It meant showing up even on the days when I felt like I had nothing left to give. It meant finding ways to add value to others' lives, even when my own life felt chaotic.

During these last few years, when people started cutting back on non-essential expenses, I had to pivot. I had to get creative about how I presented my business and I focused on educating my clients and team about the value of investing in themselves and their well-being. I showed them that even during tough times, their health and mindset were worth prioritizing.

This is what resilience looks like in action: adapting, pivoting, and pushing forward when the path is unclear. It's about believing so deeply in your goals that no obstacle can deter you. If your goal is big enough, nothing will stop you—not inflation, not doubt, not fear, and definitely not your past.

Coach's Note: Corrina didn't let her circumstances define her—she let them shape her. That's the key. Your past doesn't dictate your future. Your excuses won't pay your bills. Resilience isn't about wishing things were different; it's about doing what it takes, no matter what.

This year, life handed me another challenge, one that I never expected to face: my mom was diagnosed with Alzheimer's. Hearing that diagnosis was life-altering. My childhood had not been easy.

The emotional trauma I experienced growing up left scars that took years to heal. There were times when I resented her, times when I struggled to understand her choices and actions. But this diagnosis changed everything.

When someone you love is diagnosed with something as devastating as Alzheimer's, it forces you to reevaluate your relationship. For me, it was no longer about the past. It wasn't about the pain or the unresolved emotions. It became about doing what I knew I should— what I needed to do. Sometimes, life isn't about the things you want to do. It's about showing up and doing the things you *know* you should.

Caring for my mom now requires a level of patience and strength I didn't know I had. There are moments when the past creeps in, moments when old wounds threaten to reopen. But I've learned that resilience isn't just about overcoming your own challenges—it's about rising above them to be there for others. It's about setting aside your pain to provide comfort, support, and love, even when it's hard.

Helping my mom through this chapter of her life has been one of the most humbling experiences of my own. It has taught me the importance of forgiveness, of letting go, and of focusing on what truly matters.

Today, my team looks to me as someone who can weather any storm. They know I don't crumble under pressure. I stand tall, sort through the chaos, and come out stronger. That's because I've already lived through life's storms.

Resilience isn't something you're born with. It's something you build. Every challenge, every heartbreak, every decision carved me into who I am today. And I wouldn't trade a single one of those experiences because they made me *unbreakable.*

Raising my children as a single mom taught me more about resilience than anything else ever could. My journey has taught me that resilience is about mindset. It's about choosing growth over comfort, action over stagnation, and hope over despair.

Things I've learned and need to share so that you too are unbreakable:

1. Embrace Your Pain as Part of Your Story

Resilience doesn't mean ignoring the pain; it means acknowledging it and letting it shape you. Reflect on the moments that broke you and ask yourself: *What did this teach me? How has it made me stronger?* Your pain is not your enemy—it's your teacher.

2. Practice Radical Forgiveness

Forgiveness isn't about excusing someone else's actions. It's about freeing yourself from the chains of resentment. Start with small steps: write a letter (even if you never send it), speak to a therapist, or simply acknowledge that forgiveness is more about your peace than their apology.

3. Find Purpose in Your Struggles

Every challenge you've faced has a purpose, even if it's hard to see in the moment. Ask yourself: *How can I use this experience to help others?* Finding meaning in your pain transforms it into a source of power.

4. Build a Support System

Resilience doesn't mean doing it alone. Surround yourself with people who lift you up, hold you accountable, and remind you of your strength when you forget. Whether it's friends, family, or a coach, your tribe matters.

Imagine a life where obstacles are not feared but embraced, where each challenge strengthens your resolve. By cultivating resilience, you open the door to endless possibilities, empowering yourself to achieve dreams once thought unattainable. I don't just face challenges—I embrace them. They are why I've built a life I'm proud of, allowing me to inspire others to do the same.

"Do not judge me by my success,
judge me by how many times
I fell down and got back up again."

— Nelson Mandela

Your journey of resilience is a powerful testament to the indomitable human spirit: let it inspire others to face their fears and overcome adversity. You are UNSTOPPABLE and UNBREAKABLE!

"*You never know how strong you are, until being strong is your only choice.*"

— *Bob Marley*

LOUISE GATLAND

- Transformational Leader: Recognized for turning personal challenges into stepping stones for success and inspiring others to do the same.

- Six-Figure Income Earner: Achieved six-figure annual income within nine months of a mindset shift, proving the power of personal development in network marketing.

- Sought-After Speaker: Has spoken on stages across the USA and UK, sharing knowledge and experience with thousands through training, presentations, and testimonials.

- Resilient Business Builder: Successfully rebuilt and led a thriving team after overcoming significant setbacks, including the loss of half the organization during challenging times.

- Personal Development Advocate: Passionate about helping others unlock their full potential by fostering a growth mindset, self-confidence, and a positive attitude through personal development practices.

The Comeback Code: Fueling Success After Setbacks

The Resilience Factor

Have you ever felt stuck—like no matter how hard you work, success keeps slipping through your fingers? The frustration of rejection. The disappointment of unmet goals. The quiet voice in your mind whispering, Maybe you're not cut out for this. Life has a way of testing us, and some days, it feels like the tests never end.

But what if those struggles aren't holding you back—they're preparing you for something greater?

Resilience is what separates those who settle from those who soar. It's not about avoiding obstacles—it's about turning them into stepping stones. In network marketing, you'll face doubts that creep in when no one's looking, setbacks that shake your confidence, and moments when quitting feels easier than pressing on. The real question isn't if you'll face these moments—it's how you'll rise when they come.

I've stood in those moments. I've felt the sting of failure, the weight of self-doubt, and the fear of falling short. But every time, I made a choice: to rise, to learn, and to keep moving forward; and each time, I rose stronger.

This chapter is about unlocking that same resilience in you. Together, we'll transform your challenges into fuel for your greatest comeback. You don't need perfect conditions or endless confidence—you just need to take the first step.

Your moment is waiting. Let's ignite your resilience and make it unstoppable.

The Job That Changed Everything

November 30, 2017 will forever be etched in my memory. Losing my job wasn't just a financial setback—it felt like my world was crumbling. That night, as I stared at my phone, waves of guilt and fear consumed me. The sound of my children's laughter in the background felt bittersweet—a reminder of the joy they deserved and the weight of my responsibility to provide for them. Doubts flooded my mind: why does this always happen to me? Why am I never good enough? Why do I always let people down?

Before bed, I made a decision, albeit a small one: I'll use my network marketing business to get through Christmas, then I'll find another job. It wasn't a bold plan—just a lifeline.

But on December 1, something changed. I woke up early, feeling a fire in my belly and a sense of excitement I hadn't felt in years. There was no room for self-pity—just an overwhelming sense that I had to act. I dove into my business with relentless energy, speaking to anyone who would listen, connecting online, and sharing my story with authenticity and determination. Some nights, I worked until I fell asleep with my phone in hand.

By January, I was offered an incredible job with stability and benefits. On paper, it was everything I thought I wanted. But by then, I had a vision. I set a goal: replace my full-time income through network marketing within six months. I achieved it in three and a half months.

Coach's Note: This is where so many people get stuck. They dabble, waiting for the *perfect* moment, the *perfect* plan. But Louise's story is proof—clarity comes from action, not the other way around. The moment you go *all in*, things start shifting in your favor.

The Atlanta Convention: Seeing the Possibilities

Several months later, I attended a network marketing convention in Atlanta that would change everything. I watched my incredible upline—a mother like me—walk across the stage as a six-figure income earner. For the first time, I didn't just admire her success—I saw it as attainable for me. That moment shifted my mindset from Why not me? to This will be me.

The energy at that event was palpable. Every story shared, every milestone celebrated, reinforced one truth: resilience is what sets achievers apart. As I watched my mentor on that stage, I made a promise to myself: By the next convention, I will be standing where she is.

I messaged my husband that night: "Everything has changed. When I get home, I'm running. The goals are bigger than ever." And run, I did. Within nine months, I achieved six-figure income status and walked across the stage myself. That moment wasn't just about recognition—it was about realizing the power of resilience and belief.

The Leadership Storm: Rebuilding During COVID

When COVID-19 hit, the stability I had worked so hard to build was shaken to its core. Overnight, I lost half my team. Leaders I had mentored for years walked away. Financially and emotionally, it felt like I was back at square one. Doubts crept in: was I cut out for this? Was my earlier success just luck?

It would have been easier to quit. But deep down, I knew quitting wasn't an option. I worked closely with my coach and mentor, and together we made a pact: Even if we go back to zero, we'll rebuild with intention.

During those months, I leaned into personal development like never before. I read books, listened to podcasts, and focused on what I could control. I poured my energy into supporting the people who stayed— the ones who still believed. I held weekly team check-ins, not just to strategize, but to create a space for encouragement and resilience. Slowly, we rebuilt, and along the way, I learned that resilience isn't about holding onto what you've lost—it's about focusing on what you can build next.

Lessons and Strategies for Resilience

Every challenge I've faced became a stepping stone—a test that shaped me into the person I needed to be to achieve my goals. Resilience wasn't just something I developed; it became the foundation of my success. These pivotal moments taught me powerful lessons, and from them, I've crafted strategies that you can use to build your own unshakable resilience.

Lesson 1: Rewrite the Victim Narrative

Losing my job pushed me into self-pity, replaying thoughts like Why me? and Why can't I get ahead? But staying in that mindset wasn't going to change anything. I had to shift from asking Why me? to What now? That small change gave me clarity and control.

Resilience starts with taking responsibility for your narrative. Stop seeing yourself as a victim and start being the author of your comeback.

How to Do It:

- Reflect: Ask, What's one small action I can take today to move forward?

- Reframe: Replace thoughts like I can't with I'm learning.

- Act: Take small steps—reach out to one person or complete one task to build momentum.

Lesson 2: The Power of Belief and Vision

At a network marketing convention, I saw my upline walk across the stage as a six-figure earner. For the first time, I didn't just admire success—I believed it was possible for me. Belief eliminates hesitation, while vision keeps you focused. Together, they are the foundation of resilience, pushing you through rejection and fear.

How to Strengthen Belief and Vision:

- Create a Vision Board: Use images and quotes to represent your goals. Place it where you'll see it daily.

- Visualize Daily: Spend five minutes imagining yourself achieving your goals. Feel the pride and joy of success.

- Surround Yourself with Believers: Connect with people who inspire and support you. Their energy will fuel yours.

Lesson 3: Focus on What You Can Control

When COVID-19 hit, I lost half my team overnight. Instead of dwelling on the loss, I focused on what I could rebuild. By leaning into personal development and supporting my remaining team, we slowly rebuilt with intention.

You can't control every situation, but you can always control your response. Focusing on growth over loss creates space for new opportunities.

How to Focus on Growth:

- Set Non-Negotiables: Identify 2–3 daily actions that move you closer to your goals. Commit to them.

- Celebrate Small Wins: Recognize and celebrate every step forward, no matter how small.

- Practice Gratitude: Each day, journal three things you're grateful for to shift focus from what's missing to what's present.

Coach's Note: Most people let a setback define them. Louise let it refine her. This is what makes a true leader—when the storm comes, you don't retreat, you rebuild. What's separating the ones who *make it* from the ones who don't? Their response to adversity.

The Resilience Framework: Turning Lessons into Action

Resilience isn't just about overcoming hardship—it's about using it as a catalyst for growth. The lessons I've learned translate into actionable strategies that anyone can apply. Here's how to build your resilience step by step:

Action steps

1. Reframe Setbacks as Feedback

Failure isn't final—it's feedback. Every setback teaches you what doesn't work and moves you closer to success.

Action Step:

- Reflect: After a setback, ask yourself: What can I learn? Write down what went wrong, why, and what to adjust.

- Reframe: Replace negative thoughts like, "I failed" with, "I learned something valuable."

- Track Progress using prompts like:

  1. What happened?

  2. What did I learn?

  3. What will I do differently next time?

Overcoming Challenges:

- If it's hard to find the lesson, ask a mentor for insights.

- Use daily affirmations like, "Every challenge makes me stronger."

2. Lean on Vision

A clear vision keeps you anchored and motivated through tough times.

Action Step:

- Create a Vision Board:

    1. List three goals.

    2. Add images or quotes that symbolize them.

    3. Place it somewhere visible.

- Visualize Daily: Spend five minutes imagining your future self achieving those goals.

- Revisit Monthly: Update your board and track your progress.

Overcoming Challenges:

- If visualization feels difficult, start with smaller, past successes.

- Pair your vision with rewards for milestones.

3. Take Bold, Consistent Action

Resilience grows when you step outside your comfort zone.

Action Step:

- Identify Bold Actions: List challenging but rewarding tasks (e.g., host a live video, pitch to a mentor).

- Set Weekly Goals: Schedule one bold action weekly and commit.

- Track Results: Reflect on outcomes—what worked and what didn't.

Overcoming Challenges:

- Break daunting tasks into smaller steps (e.g., practice a live video with a friend first).

- Share goals with an accountability partner to stay on track.

Follow-Up Mechanism:

- Keep a "Courage Log" to document and celebrate wins.

4. Surround Yourself with Support

The people around you shape your resilience.

Action Step:

- Join a Community: Participate in groups aligned with your values and goals.

- Find a Mentor: Schedule regular check-ins for guidance and encouragement.

- Limit Negativity: Reduce time with people who drain your energy.

Overcoming Challenges:

- If you can't find support, start with online communities.

- Use affirmations or self-development tools to counter negativity.

Follow-Up Mechanism:

- Reflect weekly on how your environment supports your growth. Adjust accordingly.

5. Rest and Recharge

Resilience thrives on balance, not burnout.

Action Step:

- Schedule Breaks: Incorporate small breaks, like 10-minute walks or meditation.

- Find Recharge Rituals: Experiment with activities like journaling or yoga to discover what refreshes you.

- Track Energy Levels: Keep a simple log to optimize your routine.

Overcoming Challenges:

- Reframe rest as essential for productivity: "Rest fuels resilience."

- Use reminders or accountability partners to prioritize downtime.

Follow-Up Mechanism:

Review weekly:

1. Did I rest enough?

2. What boosted my energy most?

3. What can I improve?

Coach's Note: This is the playbook. Too many people overcomplicate success. It's not magic—it's mastering these five things, over and over again. The problem isn't that people don't know *what* to do, it's that they're not consistent enough to see the results.

The Key Takeaway

Resilience isn't just about enduring—it's about transforming. It's the courage to rise when life knocks you down, the audacity to rewrite your story, and the power to turn your struggles into fuel for your success.

The challenges you face aren't barriers—they're stepping stones. Every setback, every rejection, every doubt has been preparing you for this moment. Now is the time to act. Not tomorrow, not someday—today.

Close your eyes and picture the person you are becoming. The one who stands taller, leads boldly, and achieves what once seemed impossible. That person is waiting for you to take the next step, and then another. Until the life you've envisioned becomes your reality.

Resilience is a fire—it starts small, but every decision to keep going feeds the flame. Let that fire burn brighter. Let it consume every fear, every doubt, and every limitation.

You are capable. You are unstoppable, and here's the truth: the world needs your story. The lessons you've learned, the resilience you've built, and the victories you'll achieve will inspire others to rise. Your journey is proof that anything is possible for those who refuse to give up.

Your story doesn't end here. It begins now. Step into your power, light the fire, and let the world see what you're made of. Because your future isn't just waiting—it's ready for you to claim it.

Your future is waiting. Go claim it.

*"You must do the things
you think you cannot do."*

— Eleanor Roosevelt

SHANNON HOWARD

- Completed Masters of Accountancy degree in 6 months

- Rank Advanced 8 times in my first month

- Certified Life Coach

- Body Transformation Mentor

- Loving Wife & Mama

You can do Anything and be Anyone; You Just HAVE to Believe. What would you do if you knew you couldn't fail?

Have you ever paused to really think about this question? It resonates with so many of us, stirring something deep within. Would you launch a dream business, step into a leadership role, or perhaps embark on a journey to completely reinvent your life? For many, the answer is clear: "I would do more, be more, and achieve more."

So, what's holding us back? Often, it's surprising to realize that it's not a lack of resources or opportunities; it's our mindset. The beliefs we hold about ourselves shape our reality. If you perceive yourself as limited, then you will be. But here's the empowering truth: by shifting your mindset, you can transform your life. With belief as your foundation, there's no telling what you can achieve or who you can become.

In the dynamic world of network marketing, your mindset is everything. It separates those who crumble at their first rejection from those who go on to build thriving, successful businesses. When you shift your mindset, you not only change how you see yourself but also unlock possibilities you might never have imagined (and be able to empower those around you).

Coach's Note: Shannon starts off with one of the most important questions you can ask yourself: *What would you do if failure wasn't an option?* The truth is, most people don't lack potential—they lack belief. Your success will never outgrow the size of your vision. The moment you decide to believe in yourself is the moment everything starts shifting in your favor.

3 Key Aspects of Mindset

1. **Belief Shapes Reality:** The beliefs you hold about yourself directly influence your actions. If you believe you're capable of growth, hard work, and overcoming obstacles, you'll persist through challenges. Think about it: how many times have you held back from acting because you didn't believe you could succeed?

2. **Focus on Possibilities, Not Limits:** It's all too easy to get caught up in what can't be done. A strong mindset, however, seeks opportunities and views every obstacle as a stepping stone

to growth. Instead of seeing a closed door, look for windows of opportunity. This shift in focus can change everything.

3. **Positive Self-Talk and Visualization:** The way you talk to yourself matters immensely. Positive self-talk and visualizing your success reinforce your belief in your abilities, helping align your actions with your goals. When was the last time you took a moment to visualize your success? It's a powerful practice that can pave the way for your dreams.

Reflecting on my own journey, I can pinpoint a defining moment when I decided to pursue my master's in accountancy. While most people take two years to finish such a demanding program, I set my sights on completing it in just six months. It was a daunting challenge, especially as I was balancing a full-time job and cherishing every spare moment of time with my wonderful family.

Many thought I was being overly ambitious or even reckless. I remember a friend saying, "You're going to burn out!" But deep down, I believed it was possible. I envisioned myself walking across that graduation stage, and that vision fueled my commitment. With unwavering dedication and focus, I completed the program on time. We celebrated my achievement, not with a walk across the graduation stage, but with a much more memorable family trip to Six Flags—a day filled with laughter and joy that we still cherish. Our family likes to have fun!

Coach's Note: This is a perfect example of what separates those who dream from those who do. Most people would have listened to the doubts of others and slowed down. Shannon did the opposite—she doubled down on belief, locked in her vision, and took relentless action. Your success will always be a direct reflection of your ability to block out the noise and stay committed to your goals.

But my journey hasn't been all smooth sailing. Years ago, I faced a deeply personal challenge when I left an abusive relationship. I was trapped in a cycle of fear and self-doubt, convinced that I didn't deserve better. The emotional scars were heavy, and it felt like there was no way out. I knew people would judge me for "breaking up the family". Yet, the moment I decided I was worthy of love and respect was a turning point. I broke free from that toxic environment, and in doing so, I ended a cycle of pain in my family.

That decision didn't just change my life; it changed the legacy I would pass down to my children. It led me to find my best friend and husband—the partner I never thought I would find. It was because of this strong foundation of love and respect, my children are growing up with a clear understanding of what true love looks and feels like. I often reflect on how that decision, rooted in self-belief, changed the trajectory of my life and the lives of my loved ones. If you're in an abusive relationship, please know that you deserve better. Reach out for help and take the courageous step to leave—your safety and well-being come first.

Recently, I set another ambitious goal: to replace my corporate income with earnings from social retail. Initially, this dream felt distant, almost out of reach. I remember sitting at my kitchen table, staring at my laptop, thinking, "Can I really do this?" But I knew that my mindset would be crucial in making it a reality. I embraced the belief that I could succeed, focusing on positive affirmations and taking consistent steps toward my goals.

With each passing day, I'm witnessing the pieces of my vision come together in ways I never imagined. This journey of personal transformation has illuminated the incredible power of belief. When we truly trust in our potential and commit to our dreams, remarkable things can happen. If I can achieve these milestones through faith in myself, I firmly believe that anyone can realize their aspirations with the right mindset and determination.

Coach's Note: Too many people wait until they *feel* ready to go after what they want. Shannon's story proves that waiting for confidence is a losing game. Confidence comes *after* action, not before. The moment you start taking steps toward your goal—even if you don't feel ready—is the moment everything starts shifting in your favor.

However, I want to remind you that just because you enrolled in a network marketing company with your friends, it's essential to ask yourself: 'Do I belong here? Does this company truly align with my purpose?'

Having spent over 20 years in network marketing and direct sales, I can tell you that finding your right fit is crucial. I'm no longer with the companies I once represented – I had to kiss a few frogs before discovering where I truly belonged. Don't be afraid to let go of the frogs! Embrace the journey of finding the vessel that empowers you to thrive.

The Power of Mindset

The stories I've shared highlight a powerful truth: your mindset drives your success. When you cultivate a belief in your ability to achieve your goals, you open yourself up to a world of possibilities. You begin to seek solutions, embrace challenges, and persevere through setbacks. This proactive approach fuels your motivation and helps you navigate obstacles with resilience.

On the flip side, if you cling to the belief that you're destined to fail, your thoughts and actions will naturally align with that negative perception. You may hesitate to take risks, shy away from opportunities, or even give up before you've really begun. This self-fulfilling prophecy can create a cycle of doubt that hinders your progress and stifles your potential.

Ultimately, the stories I've experienced and witnessed reinforce the idea that success isn't merely a matter of luck or circumstance; it's a reflection of the mindset you choose to adopt. By embracing a positive, growth-oriented perspective, you can transform your challenges into stepping stones and pave the way for achieving your dreams.

Actionable Steps to Shift Your Mindset

Here's how you can start cultivating this mindset:

1. **Challenge Your Beliefs:** Begin by recognizing the limiting beliefs you hold about yourself. Write them down and question them. Are they really true? More often than not, you'll find they're based on fear or past experiences, not reality. For example, if you tell yourself, "I'm not a natural leader," dig deeper. What evidence do you have to support that belief? Often, you'll find that your self-doubt is unfounded.

2. **Reframe Failure:** Instead of seeing failure as a confirmation that you're not capable, view it as a learning opportunity. Every setback is a chance to refine your approach and grow. Remember, some of the most successful people in the world have faced countless failures before achieving their dreams. Embrace the idea that failure is simply a stepping stone on the path to success.

3. **Practice Positive Self-Talk:** Pay attention to how you speak to yourself. Replace negative, limiting thoughts with empowering ones. For example, instead of thinking, "I'll never be able to do

this," say, "I'm capable, and I'm learning every day." This shift in language can dramatically affect your mindset and motivation.

4. **Visualization:** Spend time each day visualizing your success. Picture yourself reaching your goals, signing up new team members, and leading a thriving business. Visualization strengthens your belief in your ability to achieve these things. Consider creating a vision board—a visual representation of your goals and dreams. Hang it somewhere you'll see it daily to remind yourself of what you're working toward.

5. **Surround Yourself with Believers:** Your environment plays a significant role in shaping your mindset. Surround yourself with people who believe in your potential and avoid those who feed your doubts. In network marketing, your community is one of your greatest assets—tap into it! Engage with supportive mentors and peers who inspire you to reach for more.

Leaning on Others

As you work on shifting your mindset, remember that you don't have to do it alone. It's okay to lean into others for support. Sometimes, we need a little encouragement or accountability to help us stay on track. Whether it's a friend, mentor, or a supportive community, don't hesitate to reach out when you need a boost.

Think about someone in your life who inspires you. Maybe it's a colleague who always seems to be on top of their game or a friend who is pursuing their passions fearlessly. Share your goals with them and ask for their support. Their belief in you can bolster your own self-belief and keep you motivated.

The Journey Begins Within

The journey to success in network marketing begins with a single, powerful step: believing in yourself. This foundational belief has the incredible power to shape your reality and propel you toward your goals. Remember, your beliefs about what's possible dictate the actions you take, the risks you're willing to embrace, and ultimately, the success you achieve.

So, take a moment to ask yourself: what do you truly believe about your potential? If you find that your belief system is holding you back, now is the perfect time to make a change. Challenge those limiting beliefs! Embrace a growth mindset and start visualizing the success that awaits you. You can achieve anything you set your mind to, but it all starts with that critical first step—believing that you can.

Your Call to Action

Now, here's where you come in. What will you do next? Share your goals with someone who inspires you, commit to practicing one of the mindset strategies we discussed, or set aside time each day for visualization. Whatever it is, take that step today. This moment can be a turning point in your journey.

Picture the endless possibilities that lie ahead when you truly believe in yourself. Embrace this moment as a launchpad for your journey. Remember, your future is bright, and it's waiting for you to step into it with confidence and determination.

So... what's your next step? Will you take a leap of faith and reach out to someone for support? Will you write down your limiting beliefs and challenge them? Will you start visualizing your success? The choice is yours, but I urge you to make it count. You have the power to shape your reality, and it all begins with a single step forward.

As you embark on this journey, remember you're not alone. Lean into your community for support and encouragement. Seek out mentorship, participate in group activities, and build connections with others who are on a similar path. Together, we can uplift each other and turn our dreams into reality.

The road ahead may have its challenges, but with a strong mindset and unwavering belief in yourself, you'll navigate those challenges with grace and resilience. Each small victory you achieve will serve as a reminder of your progress and the incredible potential that lies within you.

So, take a deep breath, embrace this moment, and step boldly into your future. You've got this!

"You are more than you are today.
You are more than
you think you can be."

— Jordan Peterson

DORA EDMONSON

- Passionate advocate for personal growth and resilience, drawing on decades of experience to inspire others to overcome challenges and thrive.

- With a deep commitment to faith, family, and empowerment, Dora has spent her life helping women find purpose and balance in every season of life.

- An accomplished author, mentor, and entrepreneur, Dora's wisdom and authenticity resonate with audiences seeking meaningful transformation.

- Known for her heartfelt storytelling and practical guidance, she empowers her readers to face life's trials with courage and grace.

- Dora's journey of faith and perseverance makes her a trusted guide for those navigating life's toughest moments with hope and purpose.

Challenges Create Champions

"Challenges are what make life interesting;
overcoming them is what makes life meaningful."

— Joshua J. Marine

At one point in my life, I felt completely overwhelmed by the constant demands of being a mother, wife, and professional. I was juggling client meetings and tight deadlines, all while trying to be present for my children and keep our home in order. I remember a particularly difficult time when everything seemed to be falling apart. My health was deteriorating, I had missed several important events in my children's lives, and my business was on the brink of failure. It was in these moments that I realized that challenges are not to be avoided—they are opportunities for growth.

Coach's Note: Dora's story is something so many can relate to—the feeling of being stretched too thin, trying to do it all, and wondering if it's even possible. But the truth is, challenges don't mean failure. They mean *growth*. The people who rise above the noise and figure out how to navigate the chaos are the ones who come out stronger.

Balancing Life's Competing Demands

Like many of you, I was searching for that elusive work-life balance, trying to give 100% at work, at home, and in my personal life. It felt like I was always falling short somewhere. But through that challenging season, I learned something that changed everything: you can't avoid the storms of life, but you can learn how to navigate through them and come out stronger.

That's what this chapter is about: turning the challenges that seem to hold us back into stepping stones toward the life we want to lead. For professionals and parents alike, we often find ourselves struggling to juggle everything—our careers, family responsibilities, personal growth, and wellness. The pressure to succeed in all areas often leaves us feeling overwhelmed and exhausted.

Embracing challenges not only helped me rebuild my business and restore balance in my life, but it has also transformed me into someone who welcomes obstacles as opportunities for growth and new beginnings.

Setting Intentional Goals

Once I understood that perfect balance was a myth, I realized the importance of setting intentional goals. These aren't just goals for my career or family but goals that align with my values, helping me create a life that feels meaningful and manageable.

To make this shift, I had to get specific about what I truly wanted. Instead of vague ambitions like "be successful" or "have it all together," I began setting clear, measurable goals that were aligned with my personal and professional vision. Whether you're working toward hitting your next rank, building a larger team, or increasing your monthly volume, setting intentional, clear goals is the key to success.

For example, instead of trying to "be there for my family" in a general sense, I set goals to spend uninterrupted time with my children each evening, even if it was just for thirty minutes. In my professional life, I stopped trying to take on every project and instead focused on the ones that matched my long-term vision and gave me energy. In network marketing, this is about more than just your personal goals—it's about creating duplication within your team. Helping your downline set and achieve their own goals creates a ripple effect of momentum that benefits everyone.

Coach's Note: One of the biggest mistakes people make in business—and in life—is setting goals that are *too vague*. Goals like *"I want to be successful"* sound great, but what do they actually mean? The more specific you are, the more likely you are to take *real* action toward them.

The Power of Time Blocking

One strategy that was a game-changer for me was time-blocking. By assigning specific blocks of time for work, family, and self-care, I gained clarity and control over my day. I vividly remember a week when my son had a huge band competition. At the same time, I had a crucial client meeting that I needed to prepare for. It felt like I had to be in two places at once. But instead of panicking, I applied my time-blocking method. I set boundaries with my work and blocked out the time to be fully present at my son's event, cheering him on during the competition, while dedicating focused time earlier in the day to prep for my meeting.

It wasn't about splitting my time perfectly—it was about intentional prioritization. That week taught me that balance isn't about having equal parts in all areas; it's about being fully present in whatever you're doing at the moment.

Here's how you can set your own intentional goals:

- Prioritize what truly matters to you: Is it your health, your relationships, your career growth? Make a list of the top three areas where you want to see growth.

- Break it down: Once you have your priorities, break them into specific, measurable goals. Instead of saying "I want to be healthier," a more actionable goal would be "I will walk for 30 minutes every day."

- Time block your day: Dedicate specific times of the day to certain tasks—family, work, self-care—and commit to those blocks to stay focused and balanced.

The Importance of Resilience

While setting goals is essential, resilience is what keeps us moving forward when life inevitably throws us off course. Network marketing can be a rollercoaster, full of highs and lows, and the reality is that you'll face plenty of "no's" along the way. The key to success isn't avoiding rejection—it's learning to embrace it. Every "no" gets you closer to a "yes."

I remember a time when I was close to achieving a major milestone in my business. I had worked tirelessly for months, but just as I was nearing the finish line, everything came crashing down—unexpected expenses, health issues, you name it. It would have been easy to quit, to give up on the goal I had worked so hard for. But instead, I leaned into resilience. I took a step back, reassessed, and broke the problem down into smaller, manageable pieces. Bit by bit, I rebuilt my momentum and, eventually, I not only achieved my goal but surpassed it.

In network marketing, this resilience is crucial. Whether you're facing a slow growth month, missed rank, or team attrition, your ability to bounce back, reassess, and keep going is what sets you apart from those who give up. Here's how you can build your resilience:

Building Resilience:

- Embrace flexibility: When things don't go as planned, take a breath and regroup. Flexibility allows you to pivot instead of crumble.

- Reflect on past challenges: Think about a time when you overcame a major challenge. What did you learn about yourself? How can that experience guide you in the future?

- Celebrate small wins: Even the smallest victories are worth celebrating. They build momentum and give you the motivation to keep going when the going gets tough.

Coach's Note: This is where most people get stuck. They think success should be a straight path, and when things *don't* go according to plan, they assume they're failing. The reality? *Everyone* faces setbacks. What separates the ones who succeed from the ones who don't is simple: they get up faster.

Overcoming Burnout and Finding Balance

Let's face it: burnout is real. We live in a world that glorifies hustle, and it's easy to fall into the trap of overworking, believing that pushing harder is the only way to succeed. For network marketers, especially those balancing full-time jobs, families, and other commitments, the grind can feel relentless. But I learned the hard way that success without balance is hollow. It's not sustainable.

When I was on the brink of burnout, I had to make a conscious decision to pull back. It wasn't easy, and honestly, it felt like failure at first. But stepping away from the constant grind allowed me to reset, refocus, and come back stronger. Here's what helped me find balance:

- Delegate and ask for help: You don't have to do everything yourself. Whether at home or within your network marketing business, lean on others. Delegate tasks, and don't be afraid to ask for support. Your team is there to help.

- Establish non-negotiables: Identify the things you cannot compromise on—whether it's your family time, your health, or your sleep. Stick to them.

- Schedule downtime: Rest is just as important as work. Schedule time for yourself, even if it's just 15 minutes of quiet reflection each day.

Building a Support System: You Don't Have to Do It Alone

Balance doesn't come from doing everything yourself. Building a strong support network has been one of the most important aspects of my journey, and it's equally vital in network marketing. Your team is your foundation. The strength of your support system—your upline, downline, and sideline—creates a culture that helps everyone thrive.

Here's how you can cultivate a strong support network in network marketing:

- Identify your core people: These are the ones who uplift you, offer honest advice, and stand by you through the highs and lows. Lean on them when you need it. This could be your mentor, upline, or trusted teammates.

- Expand your network: If you feel isolated or stagnant, take small steps to meet new people who share your values. Attend company events, plug into team trainings, or reach out to others within your company who inspire you.

- Show appreciation: Building a support network is a two-way street. Make sure you're also there for the people in your life, offering support when they need it most. In network marketing, this means recognizing the wins of your team and encouraging their progress.

Maintaining Momentum and Final Action Steps

It's easy to start strong, but staying motivated over the long term requires discipline and vision. In network marketing, momentum is key, and it often begins with you. The energy you bring to your business and your team is contagious. Regular check-ins with yourself and your goals are essential for keeping momentum alive.

Final Action Steps for Your Journey

1. Set a 30-day challenge: Choose one area of your business you want to improve. Whether it's prospecting, team-building, or personal development, commit to one small daily action for the next 30 days. For example, if you want to grow your prospect list, commit to reaching out to at least three new people each day or spending 15 minutes improving your social media presence.

2. Create a resilience plan: Write down three potential challenges you might face in the next few months. Next to each challenge, outline a few strategies you can use to overcome them.

3. Set weekly "non-negotiables": Identify one or two things that are crucial to your well-being—exercise, family dinners, or a hobby. Schedule them into your week, no excuses.

Becoming Your Own Champion

As you move forward on your journey, remember that becoming a champion isn't a destination—it's a process. It's about embracing the challenges life throws your way and using them as stepping stones to growth and success. Every setback, every obstacle, every detour is an opportunity for transformation.

Even today, as I continue to build my business and balance family life, challenges still arise. But I've learned to view them differently. Instead of seeing challenges as obstacles, I see them as opportunities to grow stronger, to reassess, and to realign with my values.

In the words of Albert Einstein, "Life is like riding a bicycle. To keep your balance, you must keep moving." No matter what comes your way, keep moving forward. The journey is not about avoiding challenges—it's about learning how to navigate through them, grow from them, and become stronger with each one you face.

Coach's Note: If there's one thing I hope you take from Dora's story, it's this—success isn't about *avoiding* hard things. It's about choosing to push through them, learning from them, and coming out *better* on the other side. Every challenge you face is shaping you into the leader you're meant to be.

Final Reflection: Take a few moments to reflect on where you are today. What challenge do you face that, with the right mindset and tools, could turn into an opportunity for growth? Write it down. Now, write one small action you can take today to start creating that transformation. Take that small action today. Whether it's sending a message, starting a conversation, or blocking time for self-care—start small, but start now.

You have the tools, the strength, and the resilience to succeed. Keep moving forward, one step at a time. Remember: Challenges Create Champions.

"Sometimes adversity is what you need to face in order to become successful."

– Zig Ziglar

KIM WARD

- Cover Feature Brainz Magazine, Dec 2023

- "Top 30 Leaders to Watch in 2024" The Silicon Review

- Host of Life by Design Podcast

- Reality Show Finalist - Play to Win - Ray & Jess Higdon

- "Top 10 Inspirational Entrepreneurs in 2025" MSN

How to Fuel Your Life by Creating Leverage in Your Business

She shouldn't have had to die in order for me to create change, but she did. Looking back, I don't know if I would have become the person that I am today if my mother had not taken her own life.

The truth is, I was numb to this kind of pain and trauma. Seven years prior, I was five months pregnant with my first daughter and my only sister, Katie, had taken her life. It was the most devastating thing that I had ever lived through, until now of course.

This time I was eight months pregnant with my second daughter and it was just three days after Christmas. At first, I was mad. *How could she? How selfish!*

Almost instantly something in me started to stir and I looked at my husband (who was Lieutenant with the local fire department) and I said, "*I'll never go back to work for someone else. I'll never trade my time to earn money just to hand that money over to someone who's raising our child just so I can work.*" It's a flawed system and that's not the definition of living, at least it wasn't for me.

If she hadn't died, I wouldn't have experienced that shift.

> *"Sometimes adversity is what you need to face in order to become successful."*
>
> — *Zig Ziglar*

Our daughter is now ten years old and she has been with my husband and I since the day she was born. No daycares, no nanny, and no babysitters—and we've never been happier.

Coach's Note: This is the kind of defining moment that creates true transformation. Kim's story is powerful because it shows what happens when pain turns into purpose. Many people experience loss and never take action, but she used it to change everything. The reality is, success often comes from these kinds of wake-up calls—the moments when you realize you have to change.

The Shift to Leverage

It's not like my mom died, I waved a magic wand, and we were living in a fairytale. Building a business that produces multiple six figures a year from nothing took a lot of hard work and sacrifice.

My husband is now retired from the fire department and works in the business I built in between his fire shifts and having a newborn at home. We travel a lot as a family, living the most wonderful experiences together.

Last year, my daughter's teacher asked me if we would adopt her because in just one school year, we traveled to London, Puerto Rico twice, and a cruise to the Bahamas. It was really cool to see my daughter wearing a full gown from the Tower Castle in London as her Halloween costume at school and humbly tell the story of where she got it.

What is it that you need more of? **Time freedom? Location freedom?**

The whole point of my contribution to this incredible book is to help you achieve those things by creating leverage.

The Question That Changed Everything

In 2020, I was working with my financial coach on a video meeting, and she leaned in and asked me a question that would shift my life and business, again.

"What would you do if you were physically unable to work your business for four consecutive months?"

That's when I realized things needed to change. I had retired my husband, but he wasn't part of our business yet. He wasn't a work-at-home dad, he wasn't a stay-at-home dad—he was a *do-whatever-he-wanted-to dad.* That meant the financial responsibility was on me to provide for our family, and it also meant if I didn't work, I didn't get paid.

I had created a job from home. **Where's the time freedom in that?** There wasn't. I was always stressed out and honestly quite miserable. If she hadn't asked me that question, it wouldn't have caused the shift that I need to share with you.

Coach's Note: This is where so many entrepreneurs get stuck—they leave a job thinking they're getting *freedom,* **but instead, they create a** *job* **they can't escape from. True leverage means** *your business works even when you don't.* **That's the real game-changer.**

Finding Leverage

For the next few days, I went down a rabbit hole of options to create leverage. Of course, I do and recommend video marketing. I'm a speaker as well, but that's really twice a year when event season is in full swing. In December 2023, I was the cover feature of *Brainz Magazine,* which was such an honor—but things like that don't provide leverage, they provide exposure.

I needed to create *my* form of leverage.

You're not ever going to believe me when I tell you what changed everything for me, but I'm going to tell you anyway.

Pinterest marketing.

I know how it sounds, but Pinterest is a very powerful search engine— it's not just a place for hair, skin, nails, and decor. Massive brands that you know and love choose to spend their advertising dollars on Pinterest, so what do they know that you don't?

I'll tell you.

There are currently over 100,000 Google searches every second (according to Google.com), and every time that you create a piece of content on Pinterest, not only does it index on the Pinterest platform where there are currently 522 million monthly active users, but your Pinterest content also indexes on Google—making your Pinterest journey evergreen and leveraged.

How It Works

People go to Pinterest to search for ideas and inspiration. When they connect with a pin that makes sense for them, they click the pin and find themselves redirected to wherever the person who pinned that piece of content wanted them to go.

Let's put you in the marketing seat for a moment. You know what your audience needs, right? You can create a piece of content called a **pin**. This can be a graphic that you create on Canva.com or it can be a vertical short-form video that you record right on your phone.

Understanding how your audience searches and what they're searching for is an important part of the process because **Pinterest is a search engine** and search engines operate based on keywords.

How to Get Started

Some of my favorite keyword tools are:

- ✓ successwithkimward.com/pininspector
- ✓ Pinterest.com
- ✓ Google.com
- ✓ Answerthepublic.com

Once you have an idea of what your ideal customers and clients are searching for, you can create your pin and pin it.

The cool thing is, **every pin requires a URL** so when your ideal person lands on your pin, if they want more, they will convert into a lead or a customer.

My husband and I wrote our Pinterest account into our will because it generates so many leads, and our cash register rings daily. That's **leverage!**

Your Action Plan

If you feel like you're ready to start your Pinterest journey, here's what to do next:

1. **Create your Pinterest account** at <u>business.pinterest.com</u>

2. **Research topics (keywords)** to support your audience and create content that answers their questions and supports their needs

3. **Pin it** and point it to a business asset—YouTube videos, podcast episodes, lead magnets, affiliate offers, digital products, or social media pages

You'll be on your way to **consistent leads and consistent sales** around the clock with this search engine that doesn't sleep.

I'll always miss my mom, and I'll always be grateful for the lessons and blessings that she left me with. Now, I get to work with my husband helping family-focused entrepreneurs build leveraged businesses so they can maximize profit *and* family time.

I'm rooting for you!

"Until one is committed, there is hesitancy, the chance to draw back, always ineffectiveness. Concerning all acts of initiative and creation, there is one elementary truth the ignorance of which kills countless ideas and splendid plans: that the moment one definitely commits oneself, then providence moves too.

All sorts of things occur to help one that would never otherwise have occurred. A whole stream of events issues from the decision, raising in one's favour all manner of unforeseen incidents, meetings and material assistance which no man could have dreamed would have come his way. I have learned a deep respect for one of Goethe's couplets:

Whatever you can do or dream you can, begin it. Boldness has genius, power and magic in it. Begin it now."

— William Hutchinson Murray

MATT HALL

- Hit the top rank in his company

- Million Dollar Hall of Fame Earner

- Team grows by 10,000+ people per month

3 Ways to Invest in Your Team for Exponential Growth

I have a belief that everyone who joins Network Marketing should be joining with me. They would be extremely lucky to be joining me. You might be thinking "Matt, why would you start this chapter with a statement of ego like that?" Take a deep breath, I'm not trying to recruit you or anyone else by saying this. I simply understand that there's a true power in posture that is magnetic. I believe a large part of why I consistently attract so many people to build our business with me is this level of certainly. This confidence isn't something I just pull out of thin air. It comes as a result of the knowledge of how much I invest into my business, and in this chapter I want you to find this same confidence.

Just imagine how your business would shift if you truly believed this about yourself. What if you could approach anyone in the world, and with absolute confidence, show them how you are the best possible leader for them. Do you truly believe that the best decision those around you could make would be joining you in your business?

In this chapter you'll find a framework for how to think about what you bring to your business. You'll find a path to real belief in yourself so that you too can grow your team exponentially month by month, year by year. Your confidence comes in part from what you personally invest into your team.

When you truly believe that you are the best leader, the best option that exists, you become a magnet for leaders and your business will consistently grow and find momentum.

One of the things I love most about Network Marketing is that the only way for someone to grow is by lifting and supporting others. If you and I are working together, the only way for me to have success, is to help you to have success. This is the most noble thing in my mind. Aren't we in the best business model in the world?

The three main ways you can and ought to invest into your teams are through time, energy and resources. People don't join you because of how cool you are, and they don't simply join you because you've had success. They will join you for the promise and the hope that you will uniquely be able to help them achieve what they want. You must show them that you are the right person to help them achieve their dream.

Now, the reasons you might believe that you're the best option will vary throughout your lifetime. Your reasons in the beginning will be vastly different from the reasons you carry when you are an established and successful leader. However, I promise, you can always find reasons why YOU are the very best option for someone.

In the beginning, you may have more time to invest, and fewer resources such as money or tools and that is okay. How do you posture yourself despite the seasonal lack of one or two of these three methods of support? As a young leader you have the ability to really harness your time and energy into one or two teams compared to an established leader who may have time freedom but must divide their time and attention amongst dozens or even hundreds of leaders. That is a real benefit of being a new leader.

As an established leader, you will have more funds to invest directly into your team by providing promotions, incentive bonuses, etc. No matter where you are in your business, you can utilize a combination of these three investing methods to support your team.

Before I go into detail for each of these three investing methods, I want to impress upon you the importance of saying YES. Your team will ask for things. They will ask for promotions, mentorship, leader calls, money, etc. They will have built up in their minds what they believe is the best possible thing for them in their business. I've learned to never say no... I always say yes to what they think they need...with conditions, of course.

You see, rarely do you actually change peoples' minds in a conversation about what they truly need. The truth is that that particular request they think they need is going to motivate them far more than what you think they need.

The important qualifying question I like to ask myself is: what conditions do I need to attach to this promotion/incentive/support in order to make it worth it for me? What level of production on their part/their team's part, would merit the level of investment (of time/ money/resources) that they think they need. This empowers you to be the leader that always says Yes, but also avoids overcommitting or investing more than you are capable of.

Coach's Note: Too many people think they need to "arrive" before they can attract great people. Wrong. You just need to know *why* you are the best option *right now*. Maybe it's because you have time. Maybe it's because you're in momentum. Maybe it's because your hunger is unmatched.

Now let's dive into the 3 ways to invest into your team for exponential growth:

Time

Time is a powerful gift you can give to your team. With time you can train, mentor, inspire, and model not only commitment but action. Show your team that you are engaged in the work of building your business. Would you want to join someone who didn't have any time for you? I wouldn't either. Yes, you may be busy, and I understand that there is a psychological reason why sounding busy might encourage someone to act urgently or see you as important. But being stingy with your time isn't going to instill belief in your new builder that you are going to take care of them.

Giving time to your team doesn't look like spending hours and hours on the phone with each leader every week. That is a massive waste of time and time is one of the three most important things you can give. Giving time is rightly modeled in responding in a timely manner, having regular check-ins, participating in events, and showing up.

In the beginning of my business, getting started in college alongside my wife, we didn't have any success to demonstrate. We couldn't pour thousands of dollars into our team with incentives like we do today. Busy with jobs and college, we still chose to sacrifice our time. We chose to spend our evenings as a newly married couple working the business together. We chose to make our dates nights our events. We chose to leave a semester of college to travel and focus on our business. My wife even left college entirely, letting go of a degree she was passionate about, to focus investing as much time into our business as possible. As you read in the Murray quote above, real commitment changes everything. Her commitment to sacrifice her time for a season truly carried us through those first years of our business.

Energy

The next investment is arguably the most powerful of the three because of the influence it can have on your leaders' hearts and minds. It is your energy. When I discuss energy, what I really mean is your focus, positivity and passion. Are you forward facing or constantly glancing backward? Are you obsessed with possibility or in a state of negativity?. Is your vision clear and bright or is it currently foggy? Are you fully committed or distracted? Your energy is everything!

Energy is the one form of investment that no matter where you are in your business, you can pour into your team in abundance. You are not limited by your schedule. You're not limited by the amount of funds you can pour back into your team. You are only limited by your own potential lack of vision, passion, commitment, and enthusiasm. Plus, these are all things you can shift immediately. You can literally choose to increase your commitment at any moment. You can increase your enthusiasm in a single breath. You might not believe that right now, and that's okay. You might be in a place in your business where you feel stagnated and it's challenging to stay positive. I promise you that your ability to train your mind to latch onto possibility, to see potential, and vision will drastically change your trajectory.

The truth is, I've never seen someone in momentum lose focus and I've never seen someone lose focus and gain momentum back. So choose to stay focused despite any ups and downs you experience. Anytime I see a leader who says something to the effect of "My business is down at the moment so I've decided to start doing part time on the side." I know immediately that their focus is reduced and they will almost never get back into momentum again. Choose to stay focused! There's a similar effect with those who constantly hop from company to company and never stay focused for a decade in one direction. Mind blowing magic happens over the long term my friends.

Coach's Note: Some people mistake "investing time" for *being available 24/7*. That's not leadership. Time should be invested *strategically*—in the people who are showing up and taking action, not just the ones who "need" you all the time.

Resources

The final investment method is resources. This includes tools, programs, incentives, unique skills, money, etc. Your willingness to provide these things for your team is essential for your exponential growth; and this includes money. I have seen many different types of leaders throughout my time in network marketing and this truly makes a difference.

Those of our leaders who were unwilling to spend money on their businesses never made it beyond the mid-leadership levels. This is an actual business, so you must treat it like one. Many network marketers believe that whatever money comes in is their own money. This mindset can only take you so far. The money I make isn't actually mine, it belongs to my business. As the business owner, I choose how much goes to support the business and how much I pay myself.

Five years into our business, we were living on our network marketing income. We had however stagnated and hadn't seen as much growth in a couple years. We decided to take massive action on our efforts in a certain market to really take things to the next level. That year we invested everything back into our business. Nearly our entire income went into incentives and shipping and bonuses for our team. It required bold courage but we saw a massive transformation in our team. That was the year that skyrocketed us, tripling our income over the next twelve months. What would you need to invest to triple your income this year?

We haven't continued investing at that same insane level, obviously, that year we basically lived as if we were broke. However we have continued to make investing boldly one of our highest priorities. Investing in your business will yield the highest return.

It is important to invest wisely. Returning to my philosophy of always saying yes. You'll have some people ask for some wildly outlandish things. Checks for promises instead of results, for example. Ask yourself, how can you say yes? Speak belief into the person by stating their strengths and why you believe in them, then adjust the plan.

Remember that resources can also mean specific skills that those on your team will have access to because they joined with you. Brainstorm unique resources you have access to that you can invest into your team.

Coach's Note: This is key. Too many people try to build a business while treating it like a hobby. The problem? You can't expect *business-level results with a hobby-level investment.*

You have your own unique strengths and skills that you can offer your team. It is time to get minutely clear on what those particular advantages are so you can communicate them effectively. Write a list of all the things that make you "the best leader for them".

Get clear on which of these three ways of investing is currently lacking in your leadership and brainstorm ways you can increase them. Are there ways you can adjust your schedule or sacrifice some activities so you can spend more time in your business? In what ways can you increase your focus and energy? In what ways can you wisely invest money, tools and skills into your team?

Coach's Note: The real question is—are you ready to step up and be the leader you want to attract? Because your team will always be a reflection of you.

"Many have attained wealth and success with only ONE sales talk delivered with excellence."

– Og Mandino

ASHLEY DAWES

- Resilient Entrepreneur: Overcame personal doubts and skepticism to transform a side hustle into a thriving network marketing career.

- Innovative Leader: Transitioned to a sustainable and duplicable network marketing system, prioritizing long-term success for herself and her team.

- Conversation Strategist: Mastered meaningful engagement using the LORD analogy (Location, Occupation, Recreation, Dreams/Destinations), fostering trust and likability in customer and team relationships.

- Top Performer: Achieved a top rank in her network marketing company within four months through strategic tools, videos, and team collaboration.

From Curiosity to Maven: My Network Marketing Transformation Journey

Hello, I'm Ashley Dawes, and this is my story of transformation from curiosity to becoming a network marketing maven.

Married for twenty one years, a mother to three wonderful children, and navigating the rollercoaster of family life, I reached a point where I asked myself, "What do I want to be when I grow up?" Little did I know, a simple invitation from a friend for a "girls' day out" would pivot my life in a direction I never anticipated. Moms understand how rare a "Girls Day Out" is, of course I jumped on the opportunity.

That day, meant for laughter and leisure, turned into my first step into the world of network marketing. The promise was enticing: earn a few hundred bucks by simply sharing products with other moms. With a $300 starter kit, I took the plunge. Despite my husband's skepticism and my own naivety about the industry, my determination was unshaken.

The early years were a blend of excitement and struggle. Treating my new venture as a hobby rather than a business, I saw minimal financial return. Yet, the joy of monthly meet-ups and the camaraderie among my peers fueled my passion. It wasn't until six years in that I began to see a tangible increase in my income, a testament to my unwavering perseverance.

Coach's Note: This is where most people give up. Six years is a long time to grind without seeing major results—but that's the reality of network marketing for most people who treat it like a hobby. The ones who stick it out, adapt, and make the shift to treating it like a real business? They're the ones who actually make it.

I came to realize the existing compensation plan and the absence of efficient systems were limiting both my group and that of my team. The cycle of spending my own hard earned money to maintain ranks and the constant pressure to ensure my team's orders were placed each month became a daunting task. It was a model that seemed unsustainable for long-term success, and definitely not duplicatable.

The turning point came when I stumbled upon a TikTok that showcased a family's lifestyle I aspired to achieve through network marketing. This encounter led me to a new opportunity that promised not just financial gain but a community and a compensation plan that aligned with my values and goals. I didn't have to build teams to succeed. I was all for this. Transitioning to this new venture was not without its challenges, as I faced criticism and doubt from my previous network. Yet, my resolve was stronger than ever.

In my new network marketing home, I found success beyond my expectations. By showing up every day, sharing my journey with weight loss, energy, and wellness products, I quickly built a massive customer pod. My story is a powerful testament to the importance of finding the right fit in terms of products, compensation plans, tools, leadership and community.

My journey from a curious newcomer to a network marketing maven is not just about financial success but about resilience, determination, and the courage to embrace change. My story is a beacon for anyone looking to make their mark in the network marketing world, proving that with the right mindset, tools, and community, success is within reach.

Embarking on this journey wasn't a walk in the park. Anyone who promises you massive success with limited effort is flat out lying to you! The decision to leave my first company was tough, but what truly tested my mettle was the decision to dive back into sharing the business opportunity. I had to conquer my MLM PTSD, a remnant of past experiences. I once read that 90% of people preferred to just share links rather than recruit. I attribute this to a lack of systems and duplication. That was my bottleneck until I cracked the code on what the top recruiters were doing: simple videos, straightforward tools, and leveraging three-way chats. It turned out to be just as easy as sharing products.

Once I hurdled over that, my team's growth skyrocketed. We hit a top rank within just four months of full commitment. Like any business, we rode the waves of highs and lows. There were moments we were on fire, hitting ranks and crushing it, and then there were slower times. People's enthusiasm waxed and waned; they got inspired, then bored, and sometimes found their spark again. It underscored a truth: every network marketer needs a hefty dose of personal development to build anything significant, from a massive customer pod to a thriving team.

Coach's Note: This is the real game—the rollercoaster of emotions, excitement, and setbacks. The ones who keep showing up even when the energy dips are the ones who win. If you only work when you're motivated, you'll never win in this profession.

My go-to arsenal for personal growth includes Bob Proctor's "Change Your Paradigm, Change Your Life" – a game-changer in my journey. But the crown jewel for any network marketer, in my opinion, is *The Greatest Salesman in the World* by Og Mandino. It's not just a book; it's a blueprint to success when followed to the letter. There are many personal development books out there, just make sure you're plugging in every single day.

One pivotal strategy that catalyzed the growth of my business was the emphasis on creating meaningful conversations. In the landscape of business, particularly network marketing, the currency of success is conversation. Mastery in guiding customers to make educated decisions through the right tools and enrolling them into your vision is paramount. This is not just a part of what we do; it's the heart of our daily operations. Allow me to walk you through this daily ritual: I allocate fifteen minutes to send out this message daily, designed to ignite a spark of connection.

Here's an example message I send to start a conversation:

Hey! I'm Ashley from Colorado, a mom of three and married for 21 years. Excited to connect and learn more about you! What's your story? (so simple)

Responses vary, but the goal remains—to keep the conversation flowing. I employ the LORD analogy to navigate through these interactions: Location, Occupation, Recreation, and Dreams or Destinations. This method not only fosters engagement but also builds a foundation of trust and likability, crucial for every one of my customer or social marketer enrollments. This approach also serves to enhance algorithm visibility, ensuring my journey and insights gain more traction on my feed.

Here is what a typical conversation looks like:

Hello there! I'm Ashley, from the vibrant state of Colorado. I'm a proud mom to three incredible kids and have been happily married for 21 years. I'm thrilled to have the opportunity to connect and dive into your story! What's your journey been like?

In the event the response is a simple *"Hi,"* *I smoothly transition into the LORD analogy, starting with L-Location. For instance, if you mention you're from Texas, I'd express genuine curiosity, "Wow, Texas! How long have you called it home?" Your answer, say "ten years," would lead me to respond with enthusiasm, "A decade? That's fantastic. You must love it there?"*

O-Occupation: "What's your professional passion there?" Upon learning there for example a dedicated fifth-grade math teacher, I'd share my admiration, *"That's remarkable! How long have you been a teacher?* She mentions "twenty years". *"Wow, shaping young minds for twenty years? You're not just a teacher; you're a hero. Math was never my strong suit, so I'm in awe of your talent."*

R-Recreation: "Outside the classroom, what sparks joy for you?" Whether it's hunting, fishing, or crocheting, I aim to find common ground and deepen our connection.

Should the conversation take an unexpected turn, I pivot towards exploring your aspirations and D-Dreams, *"Has Texas always been your dream home, or did fate lead you here?"* This opens a gateway to discussing not just goals but also cherished destinations, *"Have you ventured beyond Texas? What's the most memorable place you've visited?"* Sharing personal travel experiences can weave an endless tapestry of tales and dreams.

My ultimate advice? Dedicate at least 15 minutes a day to initiate fifty new conversations. You will witness the exponential growth of your business firsthand. If you ever get into a pickle, it happens, utilize CHAT GPT to keep the conversations going or circle back to your LORD analogy.

Remember, all business is conversation, and those who have the most conversations wins! Keep learning more about people and being consistent on your social media.

Once we've had a conversation, and only then I will circle back and see if they are interested in learning more about what I do to create income from home. This is a typical message I send out only AFTER we've had a conversation.

Hey, how are you doing? I hope you have a fantastic day! I'm reaching out to you because I'm curious do you currently keep your options open when it comes to make an additional stream of income monetizing the power of social media? I don't typically throw this out there, but you are a positive person! If I were to share with you what it is that I'm doing without it interfering with what you're already doing, would you take a peek? No big deal if not, I think you're awesome either way!

And there it all is, my biggest secret to consistency, starting conversations and popping the question. You're going to make a huge impact. I am rooting for you.

— Ashley Dawes

Coach's Note: If you're not having conversations, you don't have a business. Period. This entire profession is built on relationships, and relationships start with conversations. The people who stay in their heads and "wait for the right time" never win. Start the conversations, pop the question, and let the process work.

"Could it be that when we are bold enough to step away from our safety nets and into the 'fire' of God's call, this is when we're most likely to encounter him?"

– James Lund
– A Dangerous Faith

ALESHA LIMBO

- Made 6 figures in her first year and a half in Network Marketing

- Small business owner with her husband

- On her local school board and actively involved in numerous organizations

- Fostered 11 foster kids and adopted their oldest son

Faith-Driven Leadership: Aligning Your Path with God's Plan

A year and a half ago I found myself in a spot where I had backed myself into a corner and was no longer living a life with purpose and vision, instead I was living day by day, focusing on the moment. Now, don't get me wrong, there is nothing wrong with living in the moment and soaking up each moment, it becomes a problem when you are only living in the moment and no longer dreaming, living with intention, setting goals or dreaming big. In that moment I realized that Satan's biggest goal is not to not just take us out, but to have us sit in a complacent spot, not rocking the boat, not living with big purpose, but living in that comfort zone. That day God made it so very clear to me that if I was willing to get uncomfortable, step out big, dream big and let Him be the leader of those dreams my life would change drastically. Now He didn't say it would be easy, in fact, I can guarantee you it won't be easy, but when we step out in faith and we let Him lead us, aligning our path with His plan, watch out!!

I am a wife to my amazing husband of sixteen years, a mom to five amazing kiddos, an adoptive and foster mom, a military wife, having gone through two deployments with my husband, an active community member, a member on our local school board, involved in numerous other organization boards, a small business owner and have a master's degree in counseling. Life was and is crazy busy and I let all of that get me distracted from seeking His purpose. I let myself get comfortable in pursuing these endeavors, instead of putting His purpose for my life the center of my pursuits.

Coach's Note: This is where so many people get stuck—chasing all the "good" things while missing the God things. Busyness isn't always productivity, and sometimes the hardest part of stepping into your calling is letting go of what's "comfortable" to make room for what's truly *impactful*.

When I said yes to getting uncomfortable, yes to dreaming and dreaming big, He began to open doors. That night I was scrolling through Facebook and my friend made a post about hopping on a zoom to learn more about the company she was with. I sent her a message asking her for the link. That night I couldn't unsee the testimonies I saw and joined the team that evening! Since then, the transformation, the growth and the ripple effect from that one choice of getting uncomfortable has now changed hundreds if not thousands of lives.

What I did that night is I shifted my path, now don't get me wrong, I was already impacting lives, I was already actively involved in my community, making a difference where I went, but it was in my comfort zone, it was easy and came naturally for me. I grew up in a family that loved to serve and make a difference. We would often take a meal to someone that was sick or have a family over for the holidays that had nowhere to go or just bless someone with a gift or a hug. That is just what we did, and I was comfortable with that. But here is the big difference...I was comfortable, I was staying in a space that I knew all too well and was content, just where Satan wanted me to be. I was making an impact, but not living to the full potential and intention that God had created me for.

When we take our purpose and vision and realign it to our God-given path it will require you to move forward, stepping out of the box that you have been living in. We think that box is giving us contentment and comfort, instead it is holding us in bondage, not pushing us to live into the true power and purpose that God gave each one of us. We must make a conscious choice to become faith-driven leaders, letting God direct our steps.

So how do we do that, how do we step out of our own expectations and limitations, into God's plan and purpose? It starts with recognizing who He is and that His plans for us far out exceed our own. Jeremiah 29:11 "For I know the plans I have for you," declares the Lord, "plans to prosper you and not to harm you, plans to give you a hope and a future." Ok, but this is where it gets really fun, the next verse Jeremiah 29:12 says this "Then you will call on me and come and pray to me, and I will listen to you."

To go from comfort and ease to walking out God's plan for us we need to learn how to call on Him and seek Him. We need to spend time with Him, seek Him, pray and most importantly listen to Him. Here is the best part, when we follow His leading it doesn't mean it will be easy, or everything just falls into place, but listen to what He says in Isaiah 26:3 (NKJV) "You will keep *him* in perfect peace, *Whose* mind *is* stayed on You, Because he trusts in You." He will keep you in perfect peace through the process, through the journey, through the growth! To keep our minds stayed on Him we must keep in the center of our lives. Even in the smallest details, we put Him at the center, staying in His will and direction.

Our comfort zones are dangerous, because in that zone we limit God. We think no, that will put me in a place that won't be easy, or what happens if I fail (that is a big one for me!) or what if it doesn't go how I planned? When we live in those thoughts we limit God with our small thinking, we limit the purpose He has given us because of our small thinking! When our mind is not aligned with His purpose or when we are not focused on Him, we get so easily derailed from the bigger purpose and vision. Instead, we must take the limits off God, set our minds on Him and start imagining and dreaming again!

Coach's Note: Small thinking doesn't serve anyone. God's not calling you to be "realistic"—He's calling you to trust Him. Every leader who's built something great had to stop thinking in terms of "what if I fail?" and start thinking, "What if I'm *called*?"

On that day, when I listened to the zoom and the testimonies that I heard, I got off there and I started dreaming, imagining how different my life could be, what it would look like for my family to be bringing in extra income, to be healthy again and to be in a community that encourages growth and self-development. What possibilities and opportunities would He bring my way if I let my mind stay on Him? When I moved forward in those possibilities, dreaming big as He began to open doors that I didn't even know existed! Through dreaming

His dreams and moving forward in His direction I have seen people get their lives back through getting their health in line, stepping out in faith and growing through self-development, pushing themselves out of their comfort zone, dreaming big and changing people's lives, because I stepped out. Where would their lives be, if I wasn't willing to step out? Whose lives are not being impacted because you want to stay in that comfort zone, that limits you and those around you?

Listen to what Moses said to the Israelites, Deuteronomy 30:20a (NLT) "You can make this choice by loving the Lord your God, obeying him, committing yourself firmly to him. This is key to your life." See what has been so clearly laid before us? A choice to follow Him and live life to the fullest, but it is a choice. It is a choice that we must make daily to keep our mind steadfast on Him, to pray and listen and to obey Him.

How do we take this big picture thinking and big purpose and implement it into our daily lives? Once we understand His purpose for us, once we understand the power of walking out of our comfort zone into a place of intention and direction we must move. We must take that step, no matter how hard or uncomfortable we must move! When I decided to move in the direction of network marketing and being more intentional in my relationships and connections I had to take steps, I could no longer just sit and wait for it to happen, but I had to take action. The action leads to change and change leads to impact! That action might include pursuing that job that God laid on your heart or finishing the degree that you started or reaching out to that contact that will put you in the right room to move forward. Do you see the common denominator? It is living with intention and purpose. When you know His purpose for you, that place deep in your soul that you connect with on all levels, the one that brings you the greatest joy and makes the greatest impact, that is it! But the kicker is, it does not just happen on its own, does it? It requires you to take steps with intention, a choice to move forward.

Now, here is where it gets really fun, when we step out with intention into the plan God has for us we naturally step into the leadership role He has created for us. So oftentimes we think of leaders as being the ones that are leading the masses, or running the team, but true leaders are the ones that walk out their calling on their lives, living outside the comfort zone, because that isn't the norm! People like to be comfortable; they like to live with ease and justify it by saying well, I am content with my place in life and just need to be satisfied. So, to become a faith-driven leader, aligning your path to His plan you must step out and lead by example.

To live a faith-driven life, begin with self-reflection and awareness. Assess whether you are currently operating within your comfort zone, and identify any limiting beliefs holding you back. Articulate your purpose by writing down what you believe God has called you to do, and set specific, measurable goals that align with this vision. Make daily prayer and meditation on Scripture a priority, seeking guidance and clarity from God regarding your path. Once you have a clear purpose, commit to taking immediate action by identifying three steps you can implement today and challenge yourself monthly to step outside your comfort zone.

As you pursue your goals, embrace continuous learning and development by enrolling in relevant courses or workshops, and connect with mentors who can offer guidance. Lead by example, sharing your journey with others to inspire them and engaging in community initiatives that resonate with your vision. Regularly reflect on your experiences, celebrating successes and recognizing areas for adjustment. By stepping out in faith and aligning your actions with God's purpose, you will not only fulfill your potential but also impact the lives of those around you, encouraging them to take their own steps toward growth and purpose.

As I reflect on this journey, I urge you to consider your own path. The invitation to step out in faith isn't just about personal transformation—it's a ripple effect that can change lives around you. Each decision you make to pursue your God-given purpose and break free from the chains of complacency multiplies the impact you can have on others. So I challenge you, don't just be a bystander in your life—become the architect of your destiny. Seek your divine purpose with fervor, and run towards it with passion and determination. Remember, stepping into your God-ordained role as a leader may not always be easy, but it will always be worth it. Your journey awaits, and just beyond the horizon lies the potential to transform not only your life but also the lives of countless others who are waiting for you to take that first courageous step. Embrace the adventure, for God's plans for you are greater than you could ever imagine.

Coach's Note: The real question isn't "What if I fail?" It's "What if someone else is waiting for me to step up?" Because when you step into your calling, *you're not the only one who wins*. Your courage gives others permission to chase their own God-sized dreams.

"People don't care how much you know until they know how much you care."

— Theodore Roosevelt

EDIE LABELLE

- Seven Figure Producer

- International Speaker

- National Figure Competitor/Triple Crown Masters Figure Champion

- Multiple International Trip Earner

- Top 1% Earner

Dreams into Reality, Personal Growth Applied

Desperate housewife. That was me. A new mom, desperate for change. Back in the early 2000s, I started having kids and began losing my sense of direction. Life became an endless cycle of diapers and dishes. With three kids under three years old, including a set of boy-girl twins, I vowed to stay on top of those tasks. And I did. I became proficient at managing diapers and dishes, but I longed for something more—a bigger life for myself and my children.

While my husband had a fantastic job, our budget didn't designate one cent of "fun money." A significant portion of our income went toward future retirement and past medical debt. I had dreamt of having kids, but not like this. I envisioned traveling with them, affording activities like private lessons in dance, gymnastics, piano, swimming, and skiing—anything they might love. I wanted to be a stay-at-home mom who could bring in fabulous extra income. I knew there was more to me than just diapers and dishes. This was before social media expanded our worlds; my life felt small, but I was desperate for change and a leader to guide me.

Coach's Note: It's wild how easy it is to get stuck in survival mode, doing *all the right things*—but feeling like you're missing something bigger. The truth? You *were* missing something: a vehicle that allowed you to build, dream, and create on *your terms*. That's what makes network marketing so powerful—it's about *owning* your life, not just managing it.

Stepping Out of My Comfort Zone

One day, I met a sharp mom at the park who shared an idea that sparked something in me. She told me about volunteering at a gym to trade for lessons. Nervously, I got out of my comfort zone and negotiated a deal. My kids could take lessons at the gym while I helped coach in exchange. That small step expanded my world and gave me confidence.

At the gym, another mom introduced me to home-party-based businesses. After a few mismatches, I found a network marketing business that felt like the perfect fit. My mom became my first business partner, and I began building something meaningful. Around that time, I met a leader who accelerated my growth through a close mentorship. She encouraged me to dive into personal growth and dream big.

Early on, I read *The Slight Edge* by Jeff Olson. One of our vice presidents challenged me to sample one person a day, collect their phone number, and follow up. I accepted the challenge, making it my way of life. In my first 500 days, I met 500 new people. Many became great forever friends, customers, and business partners. Personal growth became my cornerstone, and I started reading voraciously, believing my future depended on it.

Building Dreams One Step at a Time

As I applied the wisdom from countless personal growth books to my network marketing business, I began to thrive. I climbed the ranks, earned significant income, and received numerous incentives. I created dream boards to visualize my future, and one by one, the dreams came true. I built an incredible business with incredible people, achieved massive growth, and hit major milestones.

Through it all, I remained committed to my husband and our children. I sent countless emails, text messages, and made phone calls while taking our kids to activities I could now afford. I taught them to dream big, create their own dream boards, and pursue their passions. One child became an elite travel volleyball player, another played collegiate water polo, and the third became a black belt candidate in karate.

The Power of Personal Growth

Reading dozens of books, attending seminars, and applying what I learned not only transformed my life but also allowed me to guide others. I hosted dream board nights and leadership development trainings, showing people how to achieve their dreams and build successful businesses. Personal growth wasn't just something I learned about; it became something I lived and shared.

Over time, my dreams shifted. What started as a desire for travel and financial freedom evolved into cherishing time with loved ones. I was able to care for my mother in her final days and spend precious moments with her, holding her hand to her last breath. When my father faced critical health challenges a few years later, I had the time freedom to be by his side for the entire week when he needed me most. And other joyous occasions I have been fortunate to attend that require significant time and financial investment, like my brother's PhD ceremony 2,675 miles away, and be present to celebrate countless birthdays and special occasions for the people who matter to me most. These moments underscored the true value of my journey.

Coach's Note: Money is never *just* about money. It's about choices. It's about time. It's about not having to look back with regret because *you were there* for the people who mattered most. That's what real freedom looks like—not just hitting a rank, but *building a life that aligns with your values*.

Becoming a Guide

Life gave me a guide when I needed one most, and through personal growth and persistence, I became a guide for others. I helped people put their goals on paper, create dream boards, and turn their visions into reality. Watching others shine, grow their businesses, and achieve more than they thought possible has been one of my greatest privileges.

Network marketing gave me a platform to transform not only my life but also the lives of others. By transitioning from needing guidance to providing it, I experienced the journey of a lifetime. My kids, now adults, still ask to create dream boards with my husband and me. There's power in applying lessons to real life, and it's incredibly rewarding to include the people you love in the process.

My journey from a desperate housewife to a fulfilled leader has been one of profound transformation. It began with a single step out of my comfort zone and grew into a life filled with purpose, connection, and achievement. Along the way, I discovered the power of personal growth and the joy of helping others realize their dreams. This experience has taught me that life's greatest rewards often come from pushing through fear, embracing change, and being willing to learn. As I reflect on my story, I'm filled with gratitude for the challenges that shaped me, the leaders who guided me, and the opportunities that allowed me to build a life I'm proud of.

If you're ready to start your own journey of transformation, here are some action steps to help you get started:

1. **Notice your unfulfilled dreams and create a dream board.** Spend time reflecting on what you truly want and visualize it. A dream board can serve as your constant reminder and motivator.

2. **Find a leader who is closer to your dream life than you are and be teachable.** Learning from someone who has achieved what you aspire to can accelerate your progress and keep you accountable.

3. **Develop a personal growth plan and, most importantly, APPLY what you learn.** Books, courses, and mentors are valuable, but transformation happens when you take action on what you've learned.

4. **Align yourself with people who share your vision and values.** The right community can provide support, inspiration, and opportunities to grow.

5. **Become a leader by helping someone else step out of their comfort zone and start their journey.** Guiding others not only reinforces your growth but also creates a ripple effect of positive change.

Your journey will cause a ripple effect as you positively impact the people around you. It can begin with one small, courageous step. What will yours be?

Coach's Note: The crazy part? It all started with *one decision*. One conversation. One moment where you chose to get uncomfortable. That's how transformation happens—*not all at once*, but in the daily decisions to lean in, show up, and build a life that matters.

*"A candle loses nothing
by lighting another candle."*

— James Keller

MAUREEN MESSMER

- Christian Leader Inspiring Growth and Transformation

- Military Veteran Turned Inspirational Entrepreneur

- Global Advocate for Empowerment and Community Building

Lighting the Way: How Your Influence Can Transform the World

What if I told you that one small act of kindness, one moment of forgiveness, or one word of encouragement could ripple across the world, changing lives in ways you never imagined? It's not just possible—it's within your reach. Every single person holds a candle of influence, a light that can dispel darkness and illuminate paths for others. The question is: how will you use yours?

In a reconciliation village in Rwanda, I learned a lesson about the power of influence that will stay with me forever. We arrived on a bus bumping down a dusty road, the warm African sun beating down on the landscape. As we stepped off the bus, we were greeted by young boys and girls dressed in bright colors, all smiling and dancing a traditional dance to welcome us to their village. Their joy was contagious, and their vibrant movements spoke of a culture rich in tradition and resilience. The elders stood by, watching the children with warmth in their eyes. They had prepared woven baskets as gifts for us to take home, a gesture of generosity and connection.

Then, we met two elders: Keza, a genocide survivor, and Babazi, a former perpetrator. Their stories were raw, powerful, and transformative. Babazi's voice shook, and tears welled in his eyes as he recounted the unbearable weight of his actions and his journey toward repentance. Keza's voice was soft, yet full of love and forgiveness as she described the trauma of losing her family. Listening to their stories, I fought back tears, overwhelmed by their courage and grace. Before leaving, I hugged both of them, expressing my gratitude for their willingness to share such deeply personal experiences. Their example left an indelible mark on my heart.

Keza and Babazi spoke of how Rwanda was once one people, one family, before being fractured into tribes by political and social manipulation. They emphasized how media fueled division and hatred, playing a pivotal role in the genocide. Yet, standing together, they echoed a profound truth: love, forgiveness, and unity are more powerful than division. When I asked what message they wanted me to share, their words were simple but profound. Babazi urged us to love above all else, seek forgiveness, and resist division. Keza added, "Do not divide people. Love them. Forgive them—even those who do not ask for it. We are one family."

Their story is a powerful reminder that our words, actions, and influence can either build bridges or erect walls. In a world increasingly marked by a culture of hyper-visibility, instant reaction, and division, their message is more relevant than ever. This kind of culture thrives on condemnation, but the example set by Keza and Babazi demonstrates that reconciliation and unity are not only possible but necessary for healing and progress.

Coach's Note: The weight of this lesson isn't just historical—it's *personal*. The way we lead, the way we show up, and the way we *choose* to influence others in business and life... it *all* creates ripple effects. You're either creating a culture of unity—or division. You're either raising up leaders—or leaving people behind. Your influence is your legacy.

The Power of Forgiveness

Keza's ability to forgive Babazi is nothing short of extraordinary. She lost her family, her home, and nearly her hope. Yet, through her faith and the power of forgiveness, she chose to release the burden of hatred and embrace reconciliation. Forgiveness isn't just for the person being forgiven; it's a gift to oneself. It's an act of freedom, breaking the chains of resentment and allowing healing to take root.

In our personal and professional lives, we often encounter situations where forgiveness feels impossible. A teammate may wrong us, a friend may betray our trust, or a family member may hurt us deeply. But holding onto bitterness only dims our light. As Keza showed, forgiveness doesn't mean forgetting or condoning—it means choosing love over hate. Imagine the ripple effect if we all practiced forgiveness in our homes, businesses, and communities.

Consider this: how many relationships have been fractured by misunderstandings or harsh words? How often do we hold grudges that prevent us from moving forward? Forgiveness isn't about excusing bad behavior; it's about freeing yourself from the weight of anger. In Keza's case, her choice to forgive Babazi not only freed her but also paved the way for healing an entire community.

Action Step: Reflect on someone you need to forgive. Write their name down and pray for the courage to release your resentment. If possible, take a step toward reconciliation.

The Dangers of Division

Babazi's story highlighted the devastating consequences of division. The Rwandan genocide was fueled by messages of hatred and fear, amplified by the media. While our context may differ, the seeds of division are all around us. How often do we see social media posts that thrive on public shaming and ostracism? It's quick to condemn and slow to forgive, creating an unnecessary culture of fear and isolation rather than one of understanding and growth.

We have a responsibility to set the right example for all those who watch us. More people observe us than we realize; many don't openly engage but still see what we post on social media. Our messages fill their minds and hearts and feed their actions. Instead of taking offense, we can offer understanding and grace when and where it is needed most. Words absolutely matter. We ARE influencers. The stories we share, the comments we post, and the conversations we engage in all have the power to shape perceptions and foster either division or love, teamwork, and connection.

If we don't take these steps, mistakes become magnified, and redemption feels out of reach. Yet, the story of Keza and Babazi reminds us that redemption is possible. Their journey shows that even the deepest wounds can heal when we choose love over hate and unity over division.

Action Step: Audit your social media presence. Are your posts and comments promoting unity and encouragement, or are they contributing to division? Commit to sharing content that uplifts and inspires.

Coach's Note: This is where *real* leadership shows up. Anyone can react. Anyone can criticize. But can you hold space for the messy, the uncomfortable, and the complicated? **Can you build a business and a life where people feel *safe—* safe to grow, safe to fail, and safe to rise again? That's leadership. That's influence.**

The Light You Share Multiplies

One of the most moving aspects of Keza and Babazi's story is how they now work together to rebuild their community. They understand that lighting someone else's way doesn't diminish their own light—it multiplies it. Their collaboration is a testament to the power of shared influence. By coming together, they've created a safer, stronger community for future generations.

This principle applies in every area of life. In home-based businesses, collaboration often yields better results than competition. When we mentor others, share resources, or celebrate someone else's success, we're not diminishing our own achievements. Instead, we're fostering a culture of abundance and collective growth.

Sometimes, when people become angry or distant, it's not because they don't care—it's because they do. Pain often drives behavior we don't understand. In these moments, instead of shutting them out or blocking them, we must dig deeper to uncover their needs or the hurt they feel. When we ask questions and truly listen, we often gain a new understanding of others. This understanding forges bonds and friendships that might never have existed otherwise.

Action Step: Identify someone in your circle who could use your support. Offer mentorship, encouragement, or simply a listening ear. Watch how your light grows as you light theirs.

Applying These Principles to Your Home-Based Business

In a home-based business, creating an environment that fosters growth, honesty, and connection is essential for success. Mistakes are inevitable, but they should be viewed as opportunities for learning rather than sources of fear or shame. When team members feel safe to admit errors, ask questions, and take risks, the result is a thriving, innovative, and collaborative environment.

Practicing open communication and encouraging forgiveness within your team can strengthen bonds and build trust. When individuals know they are valued for their efforts, not just their results, they are more likely to contribute authentically and with enthusiasm. As a leader or teammate, showing grace and understanding in the face of missteps sets the tone for a culture of mutual respect and support. This approach doesn't just benefit the individual; it elevates the entire team.

Vision for a Thriving Team

Imagine a sphere of influence where we approach mistakes with grace rather than judgment. A sphere where our words and efforts build bridges, not walls. A sphere where influence is stewarded to bring light and triumph to others, not darkness.

Painting the Vision

What could your business look like if we all embraced these principles? Picture a team where every member's unique strengths are celebrated, friendships among teammates flourish, and every voice contributes to a harmonious and productive atmosphere. This isn't just a lofty ideal; it's a vision you can create, step by step. By promoting forgiveness, unity, and the responsibility of shared influence, you can transform your business and those of your team into a beacon of collaboration and success.

Consider how often our social media presence impacts the way we interact with others. Are we quick to judge or slow to understand? Do we offer grace or demand perfection? In our teams and friendships, we have the opportunity to model a different way—one that prioritizes connection, growth, and mutual respect.

For those in home-based businesses, this vision is especially powerful. Your influence extends beyond your immediate circle. The way you are perceived to interact with clients, teammates, and competitors sets the tone for your business and your success. By embodying the principles of forgiveness, unity, and generosity, you can create a ripple effect that transforms not just your business, but that of your whole team.

Action Step: Identify someone in your circle who could use your support. Offer mentorship, encouragement, or simply a listening ear. Watch how your light grows as you light theirs.

Call to Action

1. Reflect on your influence: Ask yourself, "How am I using my voice?"

2. Practice forgiveness: Identify one person you need to forgive and take steps toward healing.

3. Promote unity: Share a positive message on your social media or within your community this week.

4. Mentor someone: Invest in someone else's growth, knowing that your light will grow alongside theirs.

5. Stay accountable: Partner with a friend or colleague to ensure your actions align with these principles.

As Helen Keller once said, "Alone we can do so little; together we can do so much." Keza and Babazi's powerful message to "love above all else" reminds us of the transformative impact of connection and compassion. You hold a candle in your hand, and as you light someone else's path, your own flame does not diminish—it burns even brighter. Together, we can illuminate the way forward, creating a world of success where trust, love, and unity shine through.

"Dream big, work smart, and watch your hustle turn into your empire."

– Rachel Lalji

RACHAEL LALJI

- Number one in company

- Company MVP 2024

- Documented 7 figure income earner

- Co- author of unstoppable success

- Co-host Mile High club podcast

Unleashing Your Personal Brand for Network Marketing Success

In today's world of network marketing, there's one undeniable truth: people buy from people they know, like, and trust. That means your personal brand is no longer optional—it's your greatest asset. Your brand is the magnet that attracts customers, builds teams, and sets you apart in a crowded market. It's what makes people stop scrolling and pay attention to you.

But let's be clear: personal branding isn't about logos, fancy websites, or perfectly curated Instagram feeds. It's about you—your story, your authenticity, and your ability to connect with others. In this chapter, I'm going to show you how to unleash your personal brand to dominate the competition and scale your network marketing business.

Coach's Note: Rachael hits the nail on the head here. Your personal brand is your reputation, your credibility, and your connection with people. It's what makes you stand out in a sea of sameness. If you're just posting about your products without showing who you are, *you*'re missing the entire point of social selling.

Visibility: Your Superpower in Network Marketing

Let's start with a hard truth: every day you're not showing up, someone else is. While you're busy second guessing your post, hesitating to go live, or worrying about looking perfect, someone else is out there sharing their story, connecting with your audience, and building the trust that could have been yours. If your audience can't see you, they can't trust you; and if they can't trust you, they won't buy from you or join your team. It's as simple as that.

Why Visibility Matters

1. Familiarity Builds Trust: The more people see you, the more they feel like they know you. Trust grows with consistency.

2. Top of Mind = Top of Market: When someone's ready to buy or join, the person they've seen most often is the one they'll think of first.

3. Connection Drives Conversion: Visibility allows people to connect with your story, your energy, and your mission.

Coach's Note: This is why showing up daily matters. Not when you feel like it. Not when it's convenient. *Every. Single. Day.* Whether it's a post, a story, or a live, your audience needs to see you to trust you. If you disappear for a week, don't be surprised when they forget about you.

Giving Value: The Key to Earning Loyalty

Visibility gets people in the door, but value is what keeps them coming back. In network marketing, your goal isn't just to sell—it's to serve. When you give value, you're showing your audience that you care about them beyond the sale.

What Does Giving Value Look Like?

1. Educate: Teach your audience something they didn't know. Share tips, hacks, or insights related to your product, business, or life.

2. Entertain: Make them laugh, share relatable stories, or create fun, engaging content that brightens their day.

3. Empower: Inspire your audience to take action, overcome challenges, or dream bigger.

Example: If your audience is busy moms, share time-saving tips, relatable parenting stories, or motivational moments from your own journey. When you give value consistently, people start seeing you as a trusted resource—not just a salesperson.

Authenticity: The Highest Frequency Known to Man

As Gary Brecka says, "Authenticity is the highest frequency known to man." In the world of personal branding, nothing is more magnetic than being unapologetically you. People don't want perfection—they want connection.

Why Authenticity Matters

• It builds trust: When you're real, people feel like they can trust you. • It creates connection: Your audience relates to your struggles, quirks, and imperfections. • It sets you apart: No one can copy the magic that is you.

Coach's Note: People buy energy. They buy confidence. They buy *you*. If you're faking it, they'll feel it. If you're hiding behind polished graphics and stock photos, they'll scroll past. But if you show up as *you*—messy, real, passionate—that's when people start paying attention.

Your Story: The Bridge to Connection

People don't join businesses—they join you; and your story is what turns you from a stranger into someone your audience feels they know, like, and trust.

Why Your Story is Powerful

1. It makes you relatable: When people see themselves in your story, they feel a connection.

2. It inspires action: Your journey shows others what's possible for them.

3. It creates loyalty: When people are invested in your story, they stick around for the long haul.

Crafting Your Story

Every great story has three parts:

1. The struggle: Where were you before you started?

2. The turning point: What made you decide to change?

3. The transformation: How has your life changed since then?

The Power of Consistency

Consistency is what separates those who succeed from those who don't. It's not enough to show up once or twice—you need to show up regularly, rain or shine.

Why Consistency Matters

It builds trust: Your audience learns to rely on you when you show up consistently. • It keeps you top of mind: In a crowded market, being present ensures people don't forget you. • It creates momentum: Small, consistent actions lead to big results over time.

I skipped posting for two weeks once because "life got busy." When I finally came back, someone commented, "Oh, I thought you quit." That moment taught me the importance of consistency—because if you're not showing up, people assume you're gone.

Final Thoughts

Your personal brand is your ticket to standing out, building trust, and creating a thriving network marketing business. When you combine visibility, value, and authenticity, you create a brand that not only attracts people but keeps them coming back. So show up, give value, share your story, be consistent, and remember: The world is waiting for you to shine. Go out there and build the empire you were born to lead!

"To get something you've never had, you must be willing to do something you've never done."

— Thomas Jefferson

BRENT ORWELL

- Built a seven-figure online business while raising a young family.

- Mentored hundreds of parents to achieve financial and time freedom.

- Featured speaker at global personal development and entrepreneurship events.

- Successfully balanced parenting and entrepreneurship for over a decade.

Building a Legacy: The Entrepreneurial Parent's Guide to Success

Imagine this: Your child, years from now, recalling the way you lived. Not just the things you provided but the lessons they absorbed watching you navigate life. What would they say? That you were always too busy? Or that you were someone who showed them what it means to dream big and make it happen?

This isn't about guilt-tripping you; it's about a shift. A shift I had to make. I used to believe building a legacy was all about making money, stacking assets, and ensuring my family never struggled. But here's the truth that smacked me in the face one night, standing over my kid's crib: If you're not present, you're not building a legacy—you're just keeping the lights on.

That realization changed everything. I wasn't going to settle for a trade-off between financial success and being the parent I wanted to be. I decided to build a life that let me have both. Let me tell you, it's not easy. But it's possible. If I can do it, so can you.

Running an online business while raising kids feels like juggling flaming swords. There's guilt, exhaustion, and the relentless pressure to perform—not just as a business owner, but as a parent. I've missed bedtimes for client calls and skipped family outings to hit deadlines. I'm not proud of those moments, but they taught me something crucial: the goal isn't perfection, it's presence. When you're with your family, be *with them*. When you're working, *own it*.

The shift started with structure. I mapped out my days like a battlefield strategist. Time blocking became my secret weapon. Mornings were sacred for work. Afternoons? Non-negotiable family time. Evenings? A mix of reflection and planning. This wasn't just for productivity; it was about creating clarity—for me and my family. Everyone knew the plan, and that made it easier to honor the boundaries.

Coach's Note: Structure is everything when you're balancing business and family. The best leaders are the ones who set clear expectations for both themselves and their loved ones. Time blocking isn't just a productivity hack; it's a way to ensure you're fully present in every role you play.

Next came the mindset shift. I stopped seeing myself as just a provider and started thinking of myself as a teacher. Every decision I made was a lesson for my kids. They saw me invest time and energy into growing something meaningful. They saw me stumble, adapt, and get back up. I wasn't just earning money; I was modeling resilience and vision.

Automation and delegation were game-changers. I let go of the idea that I had to do everything myself. Tools and team members handled the repetitive stuff, freeing me up for the high-value work—both in business and at home. I even found ways to involve my kids in the process. They'd sit beside me, helping with small tasks or just asking questions. Those moments were golden, turning business hours into bonding time.

But let's not sugarcoat it. There were tough days. Days when deadlines clashed with school plays. Days when I felt like I was failing at everything. On those days, I leaned into my "why." My children didn't need a flawless parent; they needed a present one. Letting them see me navigate those challenges taught them that setbacks aren't the end— they're part of the process.

Coach's Note: Your kids don't need you to be perfect; they need you to be real. The most powerful thing you can show them is how to push through challenges with grace and grit.

Over time, I saw the ripple effect. My kids weren't just observing; they were learning. They saw the value of hard work, balance, and dreaming big. They started asking questions about goals and money, and I realized I wasn't just building a business—I was building a blueprint for them to follow.

Here's the thing about legacy: It's not about leaving your kids a trust fund. It's about leaving them with tools—values, habits, and memories— that set them up for success. It's about showing them what's possible and giving them the courage to chase it.

There's also something profound about creating traditions and rituals in your family life. Weekly movie nights, Sunday morning pancake rituals, or even family brainstorming sessions about the future. These small but intentional acts become anchors for your family, creating stability and memories that outlast any financial milestone. My family's tradition of reflecting on the week over a simple dinner has not only brought us closer but has also shown my kids the importance of celebrating wins and learning from challenges.

Another major component of building a legacy is teaching financial literacy. Our kids watch us navigate the world, and what better way to set them up for success than by teaching them the language of money? Not just earning and spending, but saving, investing, and growing wealth. These lessons are seeds that can grow into lifelong habits. I've had conversations with my children about the importance of creating multiple income streams and understanding the difference between assets and liabilities. These are conversations I wish I'd had growing up.

One of the most surprising things I learned on this journey is how much children understand when we bring them into the fold. I once asked my son what he thought I did for work. His answer floored me: "You help people build better lives." It reminded me that they're always watching, always learning. Bringing them into the process doesn't just teach them about work—it teaches them about purpose.

Of course, there's the flip side of legacy-giving back. I've realized that one of the most significant lessons I can teach my kids is the importance of contributing to something bigger than ourselves. Whether it's through mentorship, community involvement, or charitable giving, these acts of service show our children that success isn't just about what we achieve—it's about what we give.

Another critical aspect of legacy-building is resilience. Our kids need to see us face challenges, adapt, and keep moving forward. They need to understand that success isn't a straight line; it's a winding path filled with lessons. When we share our struggles and how we overcome them, we're giving them a roadmap for their own lives.

Reflection has been a game-changer for me. Taking time to pause, evaluate, and realign my priorities has kept me grounded. This isn't just a solo activity; it's something I've brought into our family dynamic. We have regular check-ins where we discuss our goals, celebrate progress, and adjust plans as needed. These moments foster connection and ensure we're all aligned.

Finally, I want to talk about the power of dreaming big. As parents, it's easy to get caught up in the day-to-day grind. But when we dream big and share those dreams with our children, we're giving them permission to do the same. My kids know that my business isn't just about making money; it's about creating a life of freedom, purpose, and impact. That's a lesson that will outlive any business venture.

Another layer to this is teaching our kids the value of delayed gratification. In today's world of instant results and quick fixes, showing them the importance of patience and persistence is vital. I share stories of how I built my business, not overnight, but brick by brick. They see that true success takes time and effort, and that's a mindset they'll carry into their own pursuits.

One practical way we've incorporated this is by creating a family vision board. Each year, we sit together and outline our dreams and goals as a family. It's not just about my business; it's about everyone's aspirations, from saving for a family vacation to learning a new skill. This collaborative process not only unites us but also gives my kids a sense of ownership in our family's future.

The power of small, consistent actions can't be overstated. Legacy isn't built in one grand moment; it's the sum of thousands of little decisions. Whether it's taking the time to read a bedtime story, making space for family dinners, or showing up to their school events, these acts reinforce to your children that they matter.

Let's not forget about teaching adaptability. The world is constantly changing, and the ability to pivot and embrace new challenges is one of the greatest gifts we can give our children. When my business faced hurdles, I didn't hide the struggle from my kids. Instead, I showed them how I adapted, strategized, and came out stronger. It's these real-life lessons that will serve them far more than any lecture.

Lastly, remember to celebrate the journey. As entrepreneurs, we're often focused on the next milestone, the next win. But your children will remember the joy you brought to the process, the moments you stopped to acknowledge progress, and the pride you took in small victories. Building a legacy isn't just about what you achieve—it's about who you become along the way.

Coach's Note: The real wealth you build isn't measured in dollars; it's measured in the impact you leave behind. What kind of example are you setting? Your legacy is created in the daily moments, not the grand gestures.

Action Items:

1. **Write Your Legacy Statement:** Spend 10 minutes jotting down what you want your children to remember about you. Keep it simple but clear—let it guide your actions.

2. **Create a Structured Schedule:** Use time blocking to carve out dedicated time for work, family, and self-care. Share the plan with your family to create accountability.

3. **Automate and Delegate:** Identify tasks in your business that can be outsourced or automated. Invest in tools and people to free up your time.

4. **Teach Your Kids Through Action:** Share what you're doing and why. Let them see your wins and how you handle setbacks.

5. **Reflect as a Family:** Regularly sit down with your family to discuss goals, celebrate wins, and adjust plans. This fosters connection and keeps everyone aligned.

6. **Prioritize Self-Care:** You can't pour from an empty cup. Schedule time for your mental and physical health.

7. **Create Family Traditions:** Establish weekly rituals that anchor your family and create lasting memories.

8. **Teach Financial Literacy:** Have age-appropriate conversations about money, saving, and investing. Help your kids develop healthy financial habits early.

9. **Give Back as a Family:** Find ways to contribute to your community together, whether through volunteering or supporting a cause.

10. **Dream Big Together:** Share your aspirations and encourage your kids to do the same. Create a family vision board to visualize your goals.

11. **Celebrate Small Wins:** Acknowledge progress regularly, both in business and family life. Small victories build momentum and strengthen connections.

12. **Emphasize Adaptability:** Show your children how to handle change and challenges with grace and strategy. This skill will prepare them for life's unpredictability.

This isn't about being perfect. It's about being intentional. Balancing parenthood and entrepreneurship isn't easy, but when you align your actions with your values, it's worth it. You're not just building a business; you're building a future your kids can be proud of.

"What you focus on expands. If you are grateful for the small wins, you raise your vibration and invite more blessings into your life."

— Echoed by Esther Hicks, Rhonda Byrne, and Joe Dispenza

CHRISTINE RYDZIK

- Known for her tenacity, always figuring things out and never giving up, Christine is a master pivoter.

- Received the Rising Star Award from the HBA (Healthcare Businesswomen's Association) in her former life in Corporate America life for being a rising star within the agency she was working for

- Received the Business Blast Off Award for stepping up as a leader with her local Real Estate Investing community.

- Received the Heartbeat of the Community award several times for outstanding community service and leadership.

- Entrepreneur since 2018; still figuring it out every single day!

There is Always Something to Celebrate

Have you ever hit a wall with life? Felt like no matter what you did, things just weren't going your way? Like you were stuck in the grind, missing the magic? Just caught in a hamster wheel trying different things but the outcome wasn't changing? What if I told you that finding something to celebrate—even the smallest win—could be the key to turning it all around?

But before we dive into that, let me tell you a little about myself. I'm someone who's been through the dark season of suck and come out the other side, learning to celebrate and trust every single step of the journey. In addition to entrepreneurship, I spent years in corporate America and even worked on a Marine base, which taught me resilience and adaptability. I'm also a playful, sassy, and girly girl who believes in chasing big dreams and celebrating them all—no matter how small. My journey hasn't been perfect, but I've discovered the incredible power of celebrating life's wins—big or small—to fuel joy, confidence, and momentum, and now I'm here to help you embrace that power too!

I will never forget the moment I realized I was in control of designing a life I love! I was in my mid-20s, feeling defeated and hopeless. Nothing seemed to be working, I didn't really know how to make my dreams a reality, and life felt overwhelming. I remember sitting in the pool, reading (one of my absolute favorite things to do) a personal development book, when it hit me like a ton of bricks: I was in the driver's seat of my life, not the passenger's seat! That realization changed everything. It taught me how crucial mindset is for EVERYTHING in life, especially creation.

We all know that what we focus on expands. We live in a universe that aligns with our vibration and frequency. When I started celebrating even the little things, it shifted my whole perspective. I became excited for the small wins and focused on finding them instead of waiting for something big. When I would miss celebrating a win I felt like I was doing myself a disservice, like I was taking my progress for granted. When you focus on celebrating your wins and successes, you can't help but receive MORE wins! It really is that simple—but simple doesn't always mean easy.

Coach's Note: Christine nails one of the most overlooked success principles—momentum comes from movement, not just results. When you celebrate the process, you create a loop of motivation that keeps you going. It's the same reason people who recognize progress in weight loss stick with it longer. The same applies to business. Stop waiting for the massive wins and start building confidence with the small ones.

What Is Worthy of Celebration?

My answer? EVERYTHING. For the longest time, I only celebrated the "big" things—birthdays, weddings, promotions, moves, etc. But one day, I challenged myself to think differently. I decided to celebrate ALL my wins: the big wins, the small wins, the huge wins, and the mini wins. I stopped categorizing them into size buckets. A win is a win, and every single one is worthy of celebration.

I created a celebration ritual that was authentic and easy to maintain. Later, we'll dive into how to create a celebration ritual that works for you.

The Birth of My Celebration Ritual

Let's talk about one of my biggest wins: moving from New Jersey to San Diego, CA. This wasn't just a move; it was a massive life decision that completely changed the trajectory of my life. As a Jersey girl, I had always dreamed of living in sunny SoCal, but it felt like a far-off fantasy. When I finally made it happen, it wasn't just a win—it was proof that I could turn my dreams into reality.

I remember the day so clearly. Monsieur Gâteau, my beloved kitty cat (may he rest in peace), and I were sitting in the airline lounge, waiting for our flight. It was surreal. I ordered a glass of champagne, raised it high, and toasted to our brand-new SoCal chapter. That moment wasn't just about the move—it was about celebrating everything it represented: courage, ambition, and following through on a dream. That was back in 2013, and it sparked something that has stayed with me ever since....celebrating my wins!

Coach's Note: Christine took something that could've just been a passing moment and turned it into a *ritual*. That's what makes the difference. High performers don't just experience success—they reinforce it. Think about your own business: What small daily habits or milestones could you start celebrating that will keep you in forward motion?

Defining Your Wins

Why is it so important to define what a win means to you? Because clarity is key. When you define what success means to you, it shifts your focus and energy toward recognizing it in your life. This is a crucial step in creating a positive feedback loop—where your wins fuel your motivation, and your motivation drives even more wins.

So, what's a win or success? To me, they're interchangeable. The beauty of defining a win is that it's entirely up to YOU. There's no right or wrong answer. Wins can be personal, business-related, or both. For example, moving to a home I could afford near the beach was a massive win for me—proof that determination, hard work and vision pay off. Starting my own business was another major win, one that required courage and resilience. I started my business out of necessity after being laid off three times in six years. I knew I had to take control of my career, so I dove into real estate investing and network marketing—and that entrepreneurship decision became one of my proudest achievements, and has led to several other paths!

Wins don't have to be huge. I still celebrate small wins like getting a new client, receiving a referral bonus for recommending a service I love, or even making time for a massage. I vividly remember the pride I felt as a tween when I bought my first pair of designer jeans with my own money. When my mom's best friend complimented them, I eagerly said, "Thank you, I bought them myself!" It wasn't about the brand—it was about achieving a goal I had set for myself. My mother's friend was rubbed the wrong way by my pride and told my mother I was bragging. My mother scolded me without even hearing my side! Wild, right?! While that moment taught me to be mindful about sharing my wins with others, it never stopped me from celebrating them.

Here's something to think about: What are some wins you're too shy or bashful to share? Are there moments you're proud of but keep to yourself for fear of judgment? What about the wins you take for granted—those small, everyday victories that might not seem "big enough" but are absolutely worth acknowledging? Reflecting on these can help you redefine what celebration means to you.

Here's the key: lose judgment. Stop bucketing wins into "big" or "small" and focus on the fact that they are wins, period. Every time I receive a commission or close a sale, or meet a new client, I take a moment to acknowledge it, celebrate it, and journal it, because every success builds momentum. Take a moment to reflect on what a win means to you. Grab a pen and paper—yes, real paper—and write out your definition. There's something powerful about committing your thoughts to paper. Just try it!

Now that you've defined your wins, it's time to craft your celebration ritual. Why? Because having a go-to way to celebrate makes it easy to stay consistent. Without a ritual, it's too easy to overlook or dismiss your wins. It is crucial not to take the small wins for granted! A ritual ensures that celebrating becomes second nature—a habit that keeps you focused on the positive and fuels your momentum.

What is something you associate with celebrating? Brainstorm your ideas. Maybe it's a steak and lobster dinner, a night out dancing, buying your favorite coffee, or sleeping in on a weekend. Don't overthink or judge your answers—just write them down. All of them!

Next, go through your list and determine what's realistic for you to do regularly. It should be easy to replicate with minimal barriers. For example, a steak and lobster dinner is fabulous, but let's keep it real, it is not easy to execute on the fly! Your ritual should be something you can maintain easily because—spoiler alert—you'll be doing it often!

For me, it's champagne. For as long as I can remember, I've always kept a minimum of one bottle of champagne (or "bubbles," as I like to call it) at home. It's my go-to for celebrating anything and everything. I even make sure I have a new bottle in hand before I hope for the existing bottle. I am literally ALWAYS prepared to celebrate something! ALWAYS!!! To make this ritual sustainable, I started buying splits and single serve cans so I could toast with a single glass instead of committing to an entire bottle. When I'm not drinking alcohol, I'll improvise with sparkling water. The point is, I found what works for me, and it's easy to stick to.

Taking it to the Next Level

Once I had my ritual down, I decided to share it on social media. Let me tell you, this was WAY outside my comfort zone. At first, I didn't want to come across as bragging or boastful (especially after the designer jeans incident), so I kept the details vague. I'd post that I WAS celebrating without specifying WHAT. Over time, it became a fun way to hold myself accountable and inspire others to celebrate their wins too. And guess what? It shifted my mindset completely. Suddenly, I was seeing opportunities to celebrate everywhere—and those celebrations amplified my focus on abundance and success.

But then I realized something was missing. I wasn't tracking what I was celebrating. I was so focused on the ritual that I forgot about the reason behind it. So, I created a Celebration Journal. This special journal is reserved for documenting all my wins and celebrations. On tough days, it's my go-to reminder that I'm a total badass who has accomplished a lot. Trust me, it's a game-changer. So now it's time to go shopping for your special celebration journal! Go big, get something really special! Something that makes you smile when you look at it!

Coach's Note: There's something huge here—preparedness. **How many people actually** *prepare* **for success like Christine does? This isn't just about having champagne in the fridge; it's about expecting good things to happen. It's a** *mentality* **that creates more success. Are you preparing for wins, or just reacting to them?**

Putting It All Together

Now that you have your definition of a win, your celebration ritual, and your celebration Journal, it's time to put it all together. Here's your challenge: Reflect on the past six to twelve months and jot down EVERYTHING you wish you had celebrated. Plan one big celebration to honor these wins. Then, start fresh with today—look for one thing you accomplished that you'd define as a win. Go ahead and celebrate it now, in your own fabulous way!

Don't overthink it—just start! The beauty of this process is that it's flexible and it is yours!! You can tweak and adjust your ritual as you go, but the key is to take that first step. Celebrate yourself, because you're absolutely worth it. Trust me, once you begin, you'll discover there's so much more to celebrate than you ever imagined! As I ALWAYS say #thereisalwayssomethingtocelebrate!

"According to most studies, people's number one fear is public speaking. Number two is death. Death is number two. Does that sound right? This means the average person, if you go to a funeral, you're better off in the casket, than doing the eulogy."

—Jerry Seinfeld

TARA PAGE TRUAX

- #1 International Best Selling Author.

- Over $120 Million in sales.

- Multiple 7 figure earner.

- Trained and spoke on stages globally.

Wait, I Have To Talk To People?

I am not special. I am a small town raised, artistically introverted, empathic spirit, that cried if my mom asked me to order pizza as a child. If you would have told me back then that I would talk to people for a living, that little girl would have laughed in your face. Avoiding speaking at all costs was a mission. So much so that I used dance to express myself, and became so effective at it I made a career traveling the world as a professional dancer. On paper and in pictures my life looked like a dream, but my bank account disagreed, and after having my first child on the autism spectrum, I found myself in my thirties with over six figures of credit card debt from medical bills alone. It was the network marketing industry that brought me out of the dance studio and helped us offset the six figures of debt and create multiple seven figures of income. I was able to transform my debilitating fear of public speaking into creating millions of dollars building a global business, and successfully doing it all without peeing my pants, falling off the stage, or embarrassing myself publicly. I am confident, if I can overcome such a paralyzing fear, and turn it into one of my greatest gifts, it is possible you can do exactly the same through some simple steps, applied action and dedicated practice. So, let's get started!

Coach's Notes: Tara's vulnerability here is amazing. Most are scared to share their struggles but it is the most important way to connect with others. Her journey highlights that even those with the greatest fears can transform them into incredible strengths. Reflect on her story: What fear is holding you back right now? Could it become the very skill that defines your success in network marketing?

How Do You Do It?

First I want you to think of an experience where you worked hard for something and had massive success.

For me, that time was my years as a professional dancer. Not only do I have a BFA in Dance, which was four years of intensive study, I had sixteen years training before college and my extensive professional career after college that gave me perspective, built character and was where I learned real life skills, which included dedication, determination, discipline, preparation and practice. Every one of you has real life applied knowledge and success, which can be from any area or profession. Write one success down, and the skills you learned from it.

Next, think about a time you stepped out of your comfort zone. Get a clear picture in your mind. Feel the feeling of what you experienced. Write it down. Was it good? Was it bad? What happened? Did you die?

Asking that question alone is gold, as you could not be reading these words right now if you died! Dead people are not our target audience anyway. Last time I checked, building a team in network marketing works better with real life living and breathing humans, and we need to talk to them to make money. My goal is every one of you has confidence giving that eulogy Jerry Seinfeld talks about, and none of us bury our gifts in the ground.

One of my many uncomfortable experiences was at a Network Marketing event in Utah where instead of sharing my testimony, I said my name and froze. The words would not come out. The mic rolled out of my hands as I ran off to avoid any further humiliation. It was through this setback that I knew I needed to grow my skills. But here is the most important part of that day. I, like you, did not die. Which means we are winning, and that there is hope for us, our words and our voices too!

Now that we have proof that we can do hard things, let's move on to the skills.

The Breath

"See that line on the stage? Never go behind it. When you lean forward, inhale, and exhale when you lean back." This is the ONLY coaching I was ever given for public speaking in my entire career. Minutes later I was on stage in front of a couple thousand people for my very first keynote. Only one month after the debacle where I dropped the mic and ran, but this time a fire ignited within my voice.

When I was given the advice on where to breathe, I instantly shifted from concerned with the words I was planning to say, to dropping out of my head, and into my body. This brought me into the present moment.

Coach's Notes: Tara's advice about breathwork is a massive help. If you've ever struggled with public speaking or even a simple team call, start with this: Focus on your breath, not perfection. Practice being present and grounded—it's the foundation for connecting with any audience.

Try it. Breathe in right now into your belly. Where does your awareness shift? The more present we are in our body, the easier it is to connect to our audience, whether it is a Facebook live, TikTok, in-person event, team training or large audience keynote. When we breathe, it steadies our pace, prevents shortness of breath, connects to emotion, and makes our message more impactful. It also allows us to engage in real time interactions with our audience, so we are speaking in conversation with them, versus spewing information at them.

Read a sentence out loud, and notice the impact if you breathe in different places. Also notice your body language. Try five different places to breathe. Notice how it changes your message. Notice what feels natural. Notice what feels comfortable.

Breathing also improves the sound and tone of our voice, especially if breathing deep into the belly. And getting full breaths while speaking can create power and dynamic.

Now on the flip side, one of the biggest mistakes people make when speaking is they try to calm their nervous system and take too many deep breaths. The truth is that "anxious energy" and "excitement energy," feel the same in the body. We want that excitement channeled through our words, so we can connect with those listening, not put them to sleep! So make sure to breathe to center yourself, then use that energy to connect to our audience. Smiling can help with this too.

Coach's Notes: The idea that anxious energy and excitement feel the same is a game-changing insight. Instead of trying to erase the nervousness, Tara shows us how to channel it into authentic, impactful communication. Next time you're speaking, don't aim for perfection—focus on connection. Your energy and presence are what people truly resonate with.

Even after years of speaking in front of thousands and in multiple languages with translators, I still get present in my body by breathing deep into my belly and then my chest and then exhaling at least ten times to eliminate distractions before speaking. The more present I am, the clearer I am with my message. I can trust that the words that come out of my mouth will impact at least one heart in that room.

Which brings me to the next skill.

You Will Never Speak To Everyone, So Stop Trying! Connect One Heart At A Time!

Look around. There are people all over the place that we don't want to invite to dinner, we don't want to vacation with or that we can't stand what they post on social media. Yet we get upset when those people don't like what we have to say, or don't want to work with us! This is good news. It's called diversity! Our message is not for them, just like they are not for us. That doesn't mean you said something wrong.

But what if they don't like me? What if I say the wrong thing? What if I sound stupid? What if I sound desperate? What if they think I'm trying to make money off them? What if... (you fill in the blank), because I promise we have all had those thoughts at some point in our life, especially if you are a recovering people pleaser, like myself. So let's be real, what if they don't like you?

Well, there are people who judge you and don't like you when you're broke, right? There are people who don't like you when you're wealthy or having success, too. The truth is people are not going to like you regardless. So why not unapologetically build a legacy for your family so you can overflow into the world and serve others... one conversation at a time!

Find people. Talk to them. That's your job. That's it. If someone doesn't want to listen, move on! But don't stop talking to people! Ask people questions. Connect to how they can offset an ever-rising inflation-filled world with income that could help their family, and show them how they can do that with your words and actions.

Don't Read Your Words!

Having notes, key phrases or concepts as bullet points that keep you on track when presenting is absolutely okay! It prevents us from rambling. But DO NOT read your notes word for word or you will fall flat. It is obvious to those listening when you are reading a script and you will miss connecting to your audience. This is why I record myself speaking and listen to it back, so the stories become second nature. Land the message without unnecessary detail. Know why you are speaking. Is it to connect, communicate, create or to educate? Knowing the purpose helps keep you on track and adds value to your words.

No one wants to see polished and perfect, because humans are a beautiful imperfect mess. In fact, I make fun of myself often onstage. I mix up words, I say things that don't make sense, I've almost tripped and fell. I'm a real person! I point out my flaws so that all the other real people in the room can relate as well. It is our obsession with being perfect that prevents us from connecting. The key to building trust within sales and leadership is connection. So be real. If you make a mistake, make a joke out of it. Your mess is your message.

By being brave enough to create that space for others, it gives them space to feel supported and safe in learning, making mistakes, and growing from them.

Lastly, please rehearse. Professionals practice by doing, over and over. Take notes. Make adjustments. But don't over-rehearse. You want to be able to engage with the audience in real time and in real life. Remember, we want people to do what we do. So make it look doable. But don't be afraid to suck, we all start somewhere. Practice to be present. Don't practice to be perfect.

What Is The Worst That Can Happen? (Just a Hint, No One Died)

For some of us, the worst thing that can happen when we speak publicly is we freeze, say the wrong thing, mess up, or embarrass ourselves. Which I can agree are pretty awful having experienced many of those things myself. But nothing compared to the experience I had after I shared my voice. From people I trusted.

Through the diverse journey of network marketing, I've met people that have become some of my best friends and some who have turned out to be my worst enemies. Keynote speeches where I have shared intimate stories of my family have been weaponized for other people's personal gain. I have had to file cease and desists on people who I thought were my closest friends. I've done Facebook lives that I would eventually delete and others that have gone viral. But through it all I did not stop speaking, why? Because it's part of my purpose. It's all part of the journey. The successes and failures have all shown me how powerful my authentic message can be. I'm living proof of how words inspired from the heart, with action taken behind them, can propel massive success. Success that if I can find within myself, you can too.

So Where Do You Start?

Start now. Start with a Facebook or IG live, or host a Zoom. Invite a couple of friends over and share your product or services. Raise your hand. Speak at a networking event or share your testimony on a team call. Do the actual networking part of network marketing. Just start. From there the future is unlimited.

So, let's do this thing! The world is your stage. Your message is unique and placed in your heart for a reason. The greatest gift you have happens in the present moment, in the room where you are speaking. Be there. Breathe. Be in the moment and experience the magic happening as you show up with your authentic voice and make an impact.

Remember sometimes our greatest gifts are locked inside our greatest fears. Don't let them stay prisoner there! Call and order the pizza of life with all the toppings and then share a slice with the world. There are over 8 million people on this planet, now let's go find them and talk to them! Chances are you won't die, but you sure may get wealthy along the way.

www.ingramcontent.com/pod-product-compliance
Lightning Source LLC
Chambersburg PA
CBHW071607210326
41597CB00019B/3446